WHEN ONE RELIGION ISN'T ENOUGH

The Lives of Spiritually Fluid People

Duane R. Bidwell

BEACON PRESS

Boston

BEACON PRESS
Boston, Massachusetts
www.beacon.org

Beacon Press books
are published under the auspices of
the Unitarian Universalist Association of Congregations.

22 21 20   8 7 6 5 4 3 2

This book is printed on acid-free paper that meets the uncoated paper
ANSI/NISO specifications for permanence as revised in 1992.

Text design and composition by Michael Starkman
at Wilsted & Taylor Publishing Services

In some cases, names and other identifying characteristics of people
mentioned in this work have been changed to protect their identities.

Library of Congress Cataloging-in-Publication Data
Names: Bidwell, Duane R., author.
Title: When one religion isn't enough : the lives of spiritually fluid people
    / Duane R. Bidwell.
Description: Boston : Beacon Press, 2018. | Includes bibliographical
    references and index.
Identifiers: LCCN 2018018026 (print) | LCCN 2018041072 (ebook) | ISBN
    9780807091258 (ebook) | ISBN 9780807039885 (pbk. : alk. paper)
Subjects: LCSH: Christianity and other religions. | Spiritual biography.
Classification: LCC BR127 (ebook) | LCC BR127 .B534 2018 (print) | DDC
    261.2—dc23
LC record available at https://lccn.loc.gov/2018018026

WHEN
ONE RELIGION
ISN'T ENOUGH

For Karee,
again

CONTENTS

INTRODUCTION
or, Where I Stand   1

CHAPTER ONE
"Normal" Spirituality?   12

CHAPTER TWO
Choosing   36

CHAPTER THREE
Receiving   61

CHAPTER FOUR
Collaborating   88

CHAPTER FIVE
A Field Guide to Spiritual Fluidity   101

CHAPTER SIX
Observations, Implications, Provocations   132

A Note on Methods   149
Acknowledgments   154
Notes   160
Index   177

INTRODUCTION
or, Where I Stand

WHEN NBA PLAYER JOAKIM NOAH—a center for the Chicago Bulls—isn't on the basketball court, he wears a Christian crucifix and Muslim prayer beads. Some days he also sports an Ethiopian cross made with Tibetan Buddhist stones. "I believe in God," Noah says, "but I won't say that I'm a certain religion. I think I'm a little bit of everything." In *The Life of Pi*, a best-selling book and an award-winning film, the main character calls himself "a practising Hindu, Christian and Muslim."[1] Asked by a priest, an imam, and a pandit to choose one religion, he declines: "I just want to love God." Some well-known Buddhist teachers in North America were born and raised as Jews; one of these teachers has rewritten the Psalms from the Hebrew Bible as Buddhist prayers. During the 2008 presidential campaign, one of the most contentious questions about Barack Obama wasn't about politics but concerned religion. Taught by Catholics, taken to Christian churches and to Buddhist temples by his mother, influenced by a Muslim father who also honored animism and Hinduism, and now worshipping at a black Christian Protestant congregation—is Obama a Christian, a Muslim, an agnostic, or something different altogether? (Obama received Christian baptism, but even after his formal religious affiliation was made clear, CNN famously asked, "Is Obama the 'wrong' kind of Christian?")[2]

Religious multiplicity—the experience of being shaped by, or maintaining bonds to, more than one spiritual or religious community at the same time—is occurring more frequently in the United States and Europe. In other parts of the world, religious multiplicity has long been a norm. As more and more people transgress religious boundaries, this multiplicity becomes more visible. We increasingly encounter spiritually fluid people in public life, at school, at work, at backyard cookouts, and at the health club. Spiritually fluid people evoke prejudice and curiosity, uncover assumptions, and disrupt our typical labels; they undermine religious authority, complicate religious communities, and blur social categories. Their lives question ordinary assumptions about pure, static, and singular religious identities. Above all, spiritually fluid people spark questions: How and why does someone become spiritually fluid? Are spiritually fluid people simply confused, syncretistic, unable to commit? Are they idolaters? How should we make sense of spiritually fluid people? Do they belong in our religious and spiritual communities? What might they teach us? And what do complex religious bonds imply about our own religious and spiritual identities, practices, and commitments?

This book explores multiple religious bonds as a human experience. It describes religious multiplicity rather than evaluating it. It asks how people come to claim—or be claimed by—religiously multiple identities, practices, and lives. And it concludes that religiously multiple people belong among us. Their visibility and voices bring gifts to benefit our communities and our common life.

The lives of spiritually fluid people pulse with complexity and contradiction. One person's experience could never exhaust what it means to be formed by two or more religions. By necessity, then, this book includes contradictory voices. Those voices tell stories and make points far different from mine. I celebrate these differences.

Still, no writer can transmit another person's stories without shaping them. A retold story never comes to readers in as pure a state as when the original storyteller entrusted it to a writer. We tell stories, even other people's stories, for our own purposes. We make them do what we want. Because the stories in *When One Religion Isn't Enough* have percolated through my mind and intentions, they've absorbed meanings and flavors that weren't there at first. Even if I quote someone directly, you're not hearing the tale the way the person would tell it; you're hearing my account of the experience. This translation process scares me a bit: telling other people's tales is a privilege. They entrust their words, thoughts, and feelings to me, and I can distort these even without trying.

Nonetheless, I'm accountable to the people who shared their stories with me. I'm also accountable to readers. Throughout the book, I've tried to convey—with accuracy, responsibility, and sympathy—the voices of spiritually fluid people. I know many through friendships, research, counseling, and spiritual direction. I've also tried to convey the ideas and voices of scholars who think and write about the topic. My intention is to create a thoughtful and reflective book, one that doesn't tell people what they *should* think or experience but takes a clear stand when it seems necessary. I rarely made judgments about which beliefs or ideas are the most true or legitimate. Nonetheless, I disagree with certain voices in the book. So it seems important to clarify a few of my beliefs.

WHERE I STAND

I am Buddhist and Christian. Jesus is my savior, and the Buddha is my teacher. Jesus restores me over and over again. He gives life. He heals (although not usually all at once), and sometimes that healing can be painful. Jesus asks me to be honest with him, to be present to him, and to agree to measure my life against his. For me, Jesus is divinity con carne, holiness with meaty ribs, an ultimate reality that breathes and sweats and feels. He enables me to see and hear and feel and understand Mystery with a capital *M*, by which I mean the ultimate sources, identities, meanings, and truths that orient human lives and give them meaning. I am Christian primarily by God's action and invitation. I affirmed that identity through baptism, but I did not request or choose it. God acted first.

But it's hard for me to follow Jesus. I need a schematic, a rational step-by-step guide to waking up to Mystery. Jesus doesn't provide that. The Christian Bible, after all, isn't a user's manual or a book of rules; it's a collection of vignettes, a gathering of voices. Attempting to live like Jesus requires art, not science: he teaches with metaphors and parables, not flow charts. Jesus just doesn't provide a well-marked trail you can follow directly to your final destination.

This is where the Buddha comes in. His teaching is coherent. He provides a precise eight-step path toward awakening and an overarching account of reality, or metaphysic, that fits a Western scientific worldview. (The philosopher Alfred North Whitehead once said—somewhat too neatly, I think—that Buddhism is a metaphysic in search of religion, while Christianity is a religion in search of a metaphysic.) I am Buddhist primarily by choice. Receiving nourishment from both traditions satisfies my longing for both a metaphysic and a religion. It gives me wise teaching and loving practices, a holy relationship, and a path to awakening—sustenance I wouldn't have if I were only Christian or only Buddhist.

Yet my connection to Buddhism isn't only pragmatic or instrumental. It claims me emotionally, too; I am more apt to feel tearful or joyful when chanting at the temple than when I am worshipping in church. Buddhism changes the way I know and experience God. It broadens and deepens my understanding and experience of Christianity. Likewise, Jesus helps me understand more fully why the Buddha insisted that virtue, meditation, and wisdom must be linked. Jesus calls me to action in the world in ways the Buddha does not. I have a relationship with God; I have admiration for the Buddha.

I don't need to justify my complex religious bonds. (In fact, not needing to defend themselves is a fundamental right of spiritually fluid people.) But I do want to position myself philosophically and theologically so that readers know where my feet are planted. My stance shapes what I see in the landscapes of this book.

First, I've written this book without making a sharp distinction between religion and spirituality. They are different and yet not different, distinct and closely related. Both can be lifegiving. In general, I think of religion as the formal structures and practices that shape a community's relationship to Mystery and to the world. As such, religions carry and speak with authority to particular communities that identify as part of the tradition. Religions are public expressions of a community's values, practices, and understandings. Spirituality overlaps with religion but tends to be local and idiosyncratic. It expresses a person's way of relating to Mystery through rituals, prayers, physical movements and postures, spiritual disciplines, beliefs, values, commitments, relationships, and other ways of connecting to the sacred while running errands, raising a family, and figuring out the meaning of life. Sometimes, spirituality works through religious structures, communities, and traditions, but often it functions apart from them.

Second, I am a minister of the Presbyterian Church (USA), part of the Reformed tradition of Christianity. I am authorized to represent that tradition, and I'm accountable to it. The church trusts me to guide its people and maintain the distinct character of Presbyterian theology. I trust the church to hold me accountable and to sustain me in my own spiritual life as a follower of the Way of Jesus. I am also a practitioner of Theravada Buddhism. I have never been a Buddhist monk or novice. I do not have a degree in Buddhist philosophy, and I have no authority to represent the tradition formally. My primary teacher, the Vietnamese master Thích Pháp Nhẫn, permits me to teach *ana-panasati*—mindfulness of breathing—to others as preparation for *vipassana*, the practice of insight meditation. I do not teach *vipassana*; despite thirty years of personal practice, I am not appropriately trained and supervised to teach it to others. In my spiritual and religious life, I pray the Lord's Prayer and sit in *vipassana* meditation. I take communion, the sacramental bread and wine of the Christian Eucharist, and I take refuge in the Buddha, the dharma, and the sangha. I chant sutras and the Psalms of the Hebrew Bible. I read the Heart Sutra and the Gospel of Mark.

These practices are not contradictory. The two traditions remain distinct in my life; they do not merge or create something new but complement and inform each other. They overlap in some places, and they stand apart in others. I don't fear God's judgment for having simultaneous bonds to Buddhism and Christianity, because although the Mysteries that I know in both Jesus and the Buddha are not identical, they meet us where we are, wearing the form that best suits our desires at a particular moment or season. As the Jesuits say, God (or the sacred) is not foreign to our desires.

Third, religious multiplicity for me is not entirely a choice. I sought Buddhism, but I was drawn to Christianity. After several years of contemplation and study, I sensed a call, a draw, to Christian practice and Christian ministry. A particular Christian community confirmed and affirmed that call. I identify as Buddhist/Christian because that's what I understand God to be asking of me. I'm not worried about salvation, and I don't mind incompatible doctrines. (Doctrine is only a small part of my connection to each tradition.) The tensions between Buddhism and Christianity feed me, challenge me, and help me grasp the richness of both paths. Complex religious bonds create a life-giving dance for me. I'm still learning its steps, and I suspect the choreography will change as I age. My Buddhist/Christian life isn't simply a choice; it's a vocation, a response to (for lack of a better, more inclusive term) the sacred, and it's been shaped by the people and communities that make up my life.

Fourth, I do not believe that God is one or that all paths reach the same mountain. Religions are not different descriptions of a single reality; they describe different (and sometimes related) realities. The orishas of the Ifá tradition are not identical to Buddhist emptiness, and sunyata is not identical to the (purportedly) monotheistic God of Judaism, Christianity, and Islam. Heaven and the Pure Land, nirvana and union with God—these ideas differ. As the Dalai Lama says, Buddhist practice results in Buddhist liberation; it is not the same as Christian salvation.

Each religious and spiritual path leads to its own mountain. Each mountain connects, no doubt, to others, perhaps offering a view of peaks more distant. But the microclimate, the geology, the topography, and the view from each mountain are unique. It seems likely that diverse religions point toward (or even elicit) a variety of possible ultimate realities.

How can there be more than one ultimate reality? I'm not sure; it's a paradox. I've decided to live with that unknowing. For me, it's more important to preserve the possibility of multiplicity than to reconcile it all with a logical solution. To insist on a singular ultimate reality beyond or behind all religious expressions becomes, for me, a type of violence; it risks the erasure of real differences. It's dangerous to reduce everything to a "logic of the One," because the qualities of the ultimate "one" usually look suspiciously like the ultimate reality proposed by the tradition of the person making the claim to unity. To me it's more important to preserve diversity than to be logical (in a Western, philosophical sense). Besides, the coherence of multiple realities only seems incoherent from particular cultural or philosophical perspectives, as colleagues from Asia-Pacific cultures often remind me.

WHY THIS BOOK?

This book attempts to participate in a small way in the mending of creation. I have two goals: to contribute to abundant life and to reduce suffering. Most of the religiously multiple people in North America and Europe live in a spiritual closet. There are a few well-known examples in the academic world and in popular culture (like scholar Paul Knitter or the singer Madonna), but most keep their multiplicities to themselves. It's usually a pragmatic choice to avoid judgment and shame. When they are visible, ordinary people with complex religious bonds are apt to be dismissed as dilettantes, New Agers, or people who can't commit; they are accused of practicing "cafeteria religion"— picking and choosing from a spiritual buffet—and therefore appropriating, exploiting, and dishonoring the traditions they engage. They're seen as immature, naive, facile, heretical, and occasionally even as a danger to others.

Some people with complex religious bonds earn such pejorative labels. They engage in spiritual materialism, building their egos by collecting spiritual teachings, experiences, and practices from a variety of traditions to seem more advanced, spiritually and psychologically, than other people.[3] But in my experience, most spiritually fluid people resist spiritual materialism; they are thoughtful, passionate, and integrated. Their lives challenge the "logic of the One" that shapes most approaches to religion and philosophy in Europe and North America. A majority of spiritually fluid people don't choose religious multiplicity; they're born into it or find themselves compelled, somehow, to honor more than one tradition to preserve their own integrity. They suffer when institutions and communities demand a singular religious identity.[4]

I confess that complex religious bonds are primarily positive for me. I was born and baptized into Christianity, yet from childhood was attracted—naively and illogically at first—to meditation, contemplation, and the practices and doctrines of Buddhism and other nondual types of spirituality. Growing up as a middle-class white male in a Midwestern university town, I was surrounded by people who encouraged and affirmed that exploration, implicitly and explicitly. I know from my students, counselees, and research partners that such openness doesn't surround everyone; significant suffering can result. But that wasn't the case for me. Religious multiplicity sometimes created existential anxiety and intellectual confusion, but I haven't suffered greatly from maintaining bonds to two religious traditions at the same time. Other people are not so lucky.

I've written this book in part to reduce the suffering of spiritually fluid people. I want their families, friends, employers, coreligionists, and others to understand them better, to listen to their voices without first rejecting the possibility or morality of multiple religious bonds. I'm not making a doctrinal argument, but offering a practical description of a common human experience. I hope skeptical readers—especially those who enjoy some measure of religious privilege in our culture (meaning, primarily, mainline and evangelical Christians)—will set their assumptions aside long enough to do two things: entertain the experiences of spiritually fluid people, and imagine what it's like to live a spiritually fluid life daily.

Not everyone can or should live with multiple religious bonds. But those for whom spiritual fluidity becomes life-giving need acknowledgment, support, and welcome from both monoreligious individuals and monoreligious communities. Mystery remains too large, too complex, too playful, and too dynamic to be captured fully in words, logic, and concepts.[5] Monoreligious and multiply religious people can learn from each other by exploring the contours of the sacred together, finding ways to cooperate in mending the brokenness of our relationships, communities, and the natural world. The mending can only be partial; cracks always remain, and once-fractured places might always be weak, but that doesn't make the effort hopeless or useless.

WHAT TO EXPECT

The book you are reading avoids intellectual or academic argument. I don't have an endpoint in mind. Each chapter is like a stop on a commuter train. The stations are connected to each other, but each station stands alone, offering a particular view and playing a specific role in the local ecology, just as my experience of the San Gabriel Mountains changes from the bedroom community of Rancho Cucamonga to the small town of La Verne. So as you read the book, spend time in the places that intrigue you. Get a sense for how each place is different and how it's connected to the others.

I've tried to reflect the complexity of the topic by refusing to approach it from a single perspective. The book reflects the complexity, multiplicity, and multilayered nature of its subject. I've tried to avoid neat distinctions between the past and present, the private and communal, the institutional and popular. I've emphasized theory *and* practice, the general *and* the specific. (These things aren't nearly as separate as some might assume.) The book treats its topic as both-and, rather than either-or. At the same time, my attempts to make complex religious bonds clear and manageable will erase some of the complexity of human experience. At times, the book minimizes the conflict, the struggle, and the confrontations that can accompany complex religious bonds. Engaging in multiple religious traditions might seem easier or more harmonious on the pages of a book than it does in life. That's OK. I'm not trying to entertain or offer a scholarly treatise; I'm writing to celebrate, describe, and analyze complex religious bonds.

In general, I find religious multiplicity useful, beautiful, and good, but I also know it can harm people, traditions, and communities. Some followers of Semitic religions (Judaism, Christianity, and Islam), for example, adopt ideas from nondual and nonpersonal Asian traditions (like Buddhism, Hinduism, and Taoism) for instrumental reasons. They use these ideas to sell books, promote workshops, and develop consumer products but don't typically share the wealth with the religious communities whose ideas they've used or stolen. Likewise, followers of one tradition can distort or bastardize concepts from other spiritual traditions. This practice promotes a simplistic and inaccurate understanding of some spiritual ideas, such as Donald Trump's assumption that all Muslims accept violence or follow "Sharia law" (although what he calls "Sharia law" is a caricature promulgated by the Islamophobia industry).[6]

These issues are real and important, but they are beyond the scope of the book. Instead, I've focused on three questions: How do people come to claim (or be claimed by) more than one religious tradition at the same time? How do spiritually fluid people navigate in a world that rewards singular religious commitments? And how do complex religious bonds contribute to human flourishing? The chapters that follow offer intriguing possibilities, both for reimagining what it means to be religious and/or spiritual and for recognizing how the gifts of spiritually fluid people contribute to the common good.

CHAPTER ONE
"Normal" Spirituality?

SOME TIME AGO, my friend Eduardo invited me to meet his mother. "I'll cook," he said, "and you two can talk." The poached salmon, regal on a bed of nopales cactus flesh, was perfect for summer in Southern California. But the conversation, not the food, kept me at the table.

At nearly seventy, Fidelia is a gracious, sophisticated Mexicana. She attributes her long, lithe body to fifty years of yoga practice, first alone in the closed courtyard of the house her husband would not permit her to leave, and now as part of a tight-knit community of women in urban Mexico City, where she happily lives alone. Raised as a Catholic, Fidelia once aspired to be a nun. She still worships and prays at the neighborhood church on a weekly basis, but on a daily basis, Hinduism sustains her life. Each morning, she folds her body into the asanas of hatha yoga. Before work, she does Vedic meditation and breathing exercises. In the evening, she reads the Bhagavad Gita and other texts, attending closely to scholarly commentaries. She travels by bus to visit friends and consult her teacher at a "Hinduish" yoga center. The South Asian religious tradition centers her life every day except Sunday. Sunday is the Christian Sabbath, and she spends Sundays at church. When I ask her about religious identity, she immediately and unequivocally declares, "*Alma mía* [my soul] *es hindú, yo soy católica.*"

How can someone be Hindu and Catholic at the same time?

From one perspective, he or she cannot. In Europe and the United States, most people imagine religions as monolithic, propositional (that is, focused on logic and doctrine), and mutually exclusive: if you are *this*, you can't be *that*. I call this *normal* (or *normative*) spirituality—not because it's the best way of being religious but because it's what most of us expect. We tend to assume stable, solid boundaries between religious and spiritual traditions. Going from one tradition to another is sort of like crossing the Red River from Texas to Oklahoma: "Welcome to Taoism! You are now leaving Islam—please come back again!" You can visit another religious territory, but there's no such thing as dual citizenship. This normal or normative spirituality treats religion like a lifelong commitment, almost like marriage (but perhaps more likely to endure). If the commitment doesn't last a lifetime, normal spirituality still expects religious fidelity—one tradition at a time. You can have an address in Tulsa, but only if you sell your home in Dallas. Normal spirituality believes in religious monogamy; people must leave one religion to cleave to another, taking on a new name, a new identity, a new set of beliefs and social mores. The old life is gone; a new one begins.

But some people, like Fidelia, claim two (or more) religions at the same time. Maybe they belong to a Christian church and practice Buddhist meditation, or they grow up with a Jewish mother, a Hindu father, and an extended family that doesn't expect them to choose one tradition or the other. Or they might publicly identify as Muslim while secretly praying to Hindu gods. For rhetorical purposes, let's call this state *exceptional spirituality*—not because it's extraordinary or advanced, but because it doesn't fit expectations. Exceptional spirituality challenges ordinary assumptions about so-called normal or legitimate spirituality. It raises questions about the myth of lifelong fidelity to a single religious tradition, a myth that regards religion as a singular, authoritative voice in someone's life—a solo performance, if you will.

Exceptional spirituality values religion as a choral performance. It celebrates multiple religious voices in one person despite (what others see as) conflicting beliefs and doctrines. These conflicts cast deep shadows. We can reasonably ask, for example, how a monotheistic Catholic can also embrace the polytheism of Hinduism. Likewise, how can a Yoruba priest who communes with many spirits also practice a type of Buddhism that doesn't acknowledge the existence of gods? Exceptional spirituality accepts multiple religious bonds—connections to more than one religious or spiritual tradition at the same time—not as a logical puzzle but as possible and sometimes necessary or at least preferred.[1] For example, Christian theologian and former Catholic priest Paul Knitter says, "I'm a Buddhist Christian but also a Christian Buddhist—one persona with two religious natures or 'principles of operation.' . . . To have one without the other is to have neither."[2]

Knitter's statement can confuse and perhaps threaten people who have only encountered singular religious and spiritual identities. I was confused the first time I (knowingly) met a spiritually fluid person. I couldn't make sense of what she was telling me.

When I met Ms. Nguyen, she had arrived in the United States two days earlier from a refugee camp in the Philippines. She and her Amerasian son faced persecution in Vietnam because the boy's father was a US Navy officer. For humanitarian reasons, the US government had granted them amnesty, and a Baptist congregation sponsored their relocation from the familiar world of Southeast Asia to a dilapidated Craftsman-style bungalow in a marginal neighborhood on the south side of Fort Worth, Texas. I lived nearby and worked as a newspaper reporter. My editors had asked me to write about the Nguyens' arrival.

During the interview, our voices echoed on bare hardwood floors. The house was nearly empty: no furniture, no carpeting, no personal items, no possessions that make a house a home. At one end of the living room, a fireplace mantel extended across the wall to become the top of built-in bookshelves with leaded-glass doors. Even before unpacking clothes or shopping for groceries, Nguyen had set up an altar on the mantel. At the center she placed a faded, black-and-white portrait of Donald, her former boyfriend and her son's father. In front of him, a paper plate held a pyramid of Texas oranges donated by the church. On the left, a Buddha image sat impassively before a smoldering stick of incense. On the right, a crucifix leaned against the wall, with fresh roses in a vase at Jesus's feet. I asked about the altar, and Nguyen spoke through an interpreter: "I honor Donald, because he is my son's father. I want to find him again so he can meet his son. I pray to Buddha for good luck in a new place. Later I will pray to our ancestors. Now I pray to Jesus for guidance to help me find Donald and for power to protect my son."

I nodded. "You worship Jesus *and* the Buddha?" I asked. Nguyen smiled, and I frowned. "But how—"

Our interpreter, also a Vietnamese refugee, stopped me. "It's OK!" he said, smiling and holding my elbow. "No problem! We worship both. It's our way, our culture. No problem. No conflict. I think it's difficult for Americans to understand."

Difficult, yes, but such multiplicity surrounds us nonetheless, manifesting variously in different people's lives. As I wrote this chapter, for example, a Tibetan Buddhist lama from Singapore messaged me through Facebook that he was on his way to a Catholic church for Good Friday worship. Mormons in Salt Lake City practice Buddhist meditation.[3] Another person affirms a base of childhood Lutheranism, commits himself to Buddhist meditation, adds a pinch of Taoist philosophy from a college religion course, and simmers it over the coals of a couple of decades. A Jewish mother and Christian father might raise their children as interfaith—baptized and bat mitzvahed or bar mitzvahed as full members of both traditions (a practice the author Susan Katz Miller gleefully calls "being both"). Likewise, other people grow up worshipping African Yoruba gods alongside Jesus, G-d, and the Holy Spirit, finding out in college that some people see

religions as mutually exclusive. Others find themselves drawn
to multiple traditions at different points in their lives, lured by
Mystery itself (which some people, particularly those from a
monotheistic stance, call G-d, or the ultimate, or the numinous,
or the transcendent). These people are restless until they rest in
a combination of spiritual thought and practice—a combination
that speaks to and engages their entire being.

I think of such people, myself included, as spiritually fluid.[4]
Their religious beliefs and behaviors flow among traditions for a
day or for a season to fit the landscapes of their lives. Like a river
that incorporates various streams and tributaries—a thunder-
ing cataract in one place and a quiet wetland in another—their
spirits adapt to or incorporate multiple experiences, communities, spiritual catalysts, and other circumstances that nourish
and mold who they are at a given moment.[5] Some spiritually
fluid people recite the Shema and chant the Heart Sutra in the
same worship service. Some interpret Islam through the lens
of Hinduism, receiving new insights about serving Allah; then
they look at Hinduism through the ninety-nine names of Allah
to make sense of an infinite Hindu pantheon. I've heard worshippers chant the Hail Mary instead of Buddhist sutras during
a communal, animistic ritual intended to heal their Catholic
priest of cancer. The ceremony included gongs, bowing, and
the historically animistic and Buddhist practice of holy string
infused with the power of the prayer and later worn around the
worshippers' wrists for protection and blessing. Religious mixing like this isn't new; it has been going on for a long time. The
first North American Jubu, or Jewish Buddhist, self-identified
in 1893.[6] In 1979, Benedictine nuns in Oklahoma established
a Hindu-Christian ashram, which has since become an interspiritual retreat. In Dallas, the Maria Kannon Zen Center is
dedicated both to Mary, the mother of Jesus, and to Kannon,
the Buddhist bodhisattva, or saint, of compassion.

Exceptional? Or normal?

EXCEPTIONAL OR NORMAL?

Simplistic categories like *exceptional* and *normal* don't capture the complexity of human spirituality and religious understanding, of course.[7] Religion and spirituality are amorphous and ambiguous, dimensions of life that don't—and shouldn't—fit into neat, binary categories. They're historically conditioned. My idea of *normal* spirituality—that religions are mutually exclusive and therefore antagonistic—came to the fore of religious thinking in the West as an artifact of modernity. Before modernity, many Christians presumed not only that it was fine to incorporate pagan elements into Christian belief and practice but also that non-Christians could be saved. The Italian missionary Ippolito Desideri, for instance, traveled to Tibet in 1716. He argued that Buddhists in Tibet might deny the existence of God but could nonetheless—because they had religious belief and followed a moral order—be implicitly Christian and therefore receive Christian salvation.[8]

I don't want to create a hierarchy or false dichotomy, then, between normal and exceptional religion. But by temporarily placing them at opposite ends of a continuum, we can clarify the criteria we use for what's normal, healthful, or acceptable spirituality and what's not. The juxtaposition of normal and exceptional helps us see the tensions created when common assumptions about religion and spirituality—things we've accepted as true or valid without really reflecting on them—conflict with our own ways of experiencing, identifying, and naming the transcendent, ultimate, or numinous facets of human experience and of life itself. Our connection with these elements is what I call Mystery. (Marie Romo, a Hindu Catholic woman we meet in chapter 2, calls these facets of life "the Mysteries"; for her, even the ultimate is multiple.)

At its best, the tension between normal and exceptional spirituality can be creative and life-giving, helping humans flourish.

More often it leads to conflict in families, communities, institutions, and individuals. Normal spirituality carries so much power and privilege, shaping daily life so thoroughly and yet almost invisibly, that it erases exceptional spirituality. Even when exceptional spirituality isn't erased, it's forced below the threshold of public awareness, invisible to those who don't accept it or have never considered the possibility.

EXCEPTIONAL *AND* NORMAL

The spiritually fluid people I have described so far are not isolated examples of a tiny community; they are the tip of the proverbial iceberg. Religious multiplicity increases day by day across countries and continents.[9] One-third of US marriages are interfaith; by default, these families and their children are part of more than one religious community. Millions of Christians, Jews, and Muslims integrate Hindu practices of yoga and Buddhist practices of meditation into their daily lives. Nearly one-third of US residents report worshipping in more than one religious tradition for reasons other than traveling, an interfaith marriage, or a special occasion like a wedding or funeral. Black Protestants are more likely than anyone else to attend worship in a faith tradition other than their own. Thirteen percent of US residents—one in eight—say Buddhism influences their daily spirituality, even though less than 1 percent of the US population identify as Buddhist.[10] Public school teachers instruct religiously multiple children, and judges officiate at the marriages of spiritually fluid people. Physicians navigate the ethical and doctrinal beliefs of such patients, and religious leaders worship with, counsel, and teach people who embody multiple religious traditions. Clergy officiate at spiritually fluid birth celebrations, funerals, and coming-of-age rituals. Scholars increasingly study and write about "multiple religious belonging," "complex religious identities," "dual practitioners," and "multiple religious bonds." The World Council of Churches and the United Church of Christ held an international meeting on multiple religious belonging in 2015 to begin discerning how Christian leaders should respond to spiritually fluid people in their congregations.

Most people, in fact, are spiritually fluid to one degree or another, even those who identify with one tradition.[11] All religions borrow from the cultures and forms of spirituality that surround and precede them, and these imported ideas and practices eventually seem natural. For example, Jews were the first Semitic people to bow in prayer, and Christians and Muslims adopted the practice from them. In this and many other ways, religion can be singular in name but multiple in practice, sometimes without recognition. Korean Christians, for example, are heavily shaped by Confucian ideals. A white elder in a Christian congregation in the American South believes in reincarnation. Images of Jesus stand proudly on some Hindu and Buddhist altars. Christians, Jews, Buddhists, and Muslims all use prayer beads. Jews in the United States decorate Christmas trees, and Chinese and Japanese Christians venerate ancestors at home altars.

All of this suggests that exceptional spirituality is less remarkable than we think. Despite dominant ideas about spiritual monogamy or lifelong allegiance to one religious or spiritual tradition, religious multiplicity isn't uncommon or impossible. It exists, and if it hasn't arrived in your life already, it's coming soon to a neighborhood (or family member) near you. Yet spiritually fluid people remain almost invisible outside academic conversations. They exist at the edges of spiritual and religious communities, erased from public view and rarely heard in public conversations about religion. What keeps them from boldly claiming their religious multiplicity as a gift, an identity, a legitimate way to live out spiritual beliefs, identities, and practices? Why do they seem so exceptional?

RISKS AND PRIVILEGES

Several years ago, I attended a lecture by a Buddhist-Christian scholar. After his presentation, a woman at my table leaned over to whisper, "I have to confess, I just don't get it. Maybe it's because I'm Catholic, but I don't know how someone can be Buddhist *and* Christian."

"I think of myself as Buddhist/Christian, too," I said. She looked at me for a few seconds and frowned.

"How can that be?" she asked. "I mean, if you're a Buddhist, what do you do with Jesus?"

"I don't do anything with Jesus," I said. "Jesus does things with me."

She didn't interact with me for the rest of the afternoon.

Spiritually fluid people seem exceptional because cultural conversations in North America, Europe, and parts of the Asia-Pacific region position them that way. Public conversations tend to frame spiritually fluid people as privileged, subversive, or both—an attitude that keeps religious multiplicity out of the public eye. Many factors shape this dynamic, but two are especially important: the academic study of religious multiplicity and the personal, institutional, and sociopolitical risks of violating religious and social mores. First, academic discourse tends to frame religious multiplicity as exotic, elite, and rare and therefore distant from what most think of as ordinary. Second, because it can be dangerous to violate family, community, and institutional expectations of normal spirituality, some spiritually fluid people—especially those bonded *voluntarily* to two or more traditions—fail to identify publicly as religiously multiple.[12] As a result, their experiences remain invisible to those closest to them. In trying to understand religious multiplicity, we need to give each factor a closer look.

ACADEMIC STUDY OF RELIGIOUS MULTIPLICITY

Scholars have studied religious multiplicity for years, with increasing attention in the past decade. Most of this academic work focuses on concepts. Instead of exploring what it's like to live a spiritually fluid life, scholars assess the possibility of religious multiplicity. They debate whether multiplicity can be logical, how well it fits each religion's doctrinal or philosophical system, and if and how spiritually fluid people can practice in ways that preserve each tradition's integrity without compromising essential beliefs or perspectives. These scholars tend to speak from particular theological perspectives (usually Christian). They evaluate the logical and doctrinal possibility of religious multiplicity without first adequately describing or understanding it as human experience. Much of this writing assumes a normal spirituality, especially the ideas that (a) religious traditions have clear boundaries, (b) religions are primarily focused on doctrine, and (c) conflicting spiritual or theological perspectives must be reconciled. Some scholars argue that without logical coherence, religious multiplicity is simply syncretism or cafeteria religion, in which people mix and match elements of religious traditions with no concern that the interpretations and practices preserve a tradition's integrity.

I am grateful for this scholarship, which is critical, rigorous, and thoughtful. It seeks to make intellectual sense of religious multiplicity in light of particular criteria, and it makes valuable, even essential, contributions to our understanding of religious multiplicity. But it isn't sufficient. Considered alone, this scholarship cannot illuminate the totality of religious multiplicity, because it prioritizes institutions, logic, and systems of thought over people; it measures spiritually fluid people against systems of religious thought rather than assessing religious systems in light of the varied ways people experience religious multiplicity.

As a scholar and theologian, I think existing scholarship

about religious multiplicity has at least three limitations. First, it hasn't sufficiently understood religious multiplicity as experienced in daily life by spiritually fluid people. There is a great need for qualitative research into religious multiplicity, including ethnographies, narrative analyses, and the development of grounded theory. This research should privilege and be accountable to the lives of spiritually fluid people.

Second, academic study has taken a primarily cognitive approach to religious multiplicity, as if religion were solely about belief or doctrine. A focus on doctrine or "orthodoxy" cannot account adequately for how spiritually fluid people integrate and practice their religions through bodies, minds, communities, values, rituals, traditions, and ordinary behaviors. In their daily practices, spiritually fluid people often hold opposites together in ways that intellect and logic cannot. We shouldn't reduce religious multiplicity to questions of cohesive doctrine versus conflicting doctrine or to rational propositions about reality.

Third, scholars tend to frame religious multiplicity as a cognitive choice made by educated, socially privileged (and usually white) people. They assume that religious multiplicity is always, or mostly, voluntary. As a result, they focus on people that British theologian Rose Drew calls "elite practitioners," or spiritually fluid people who have the freedom, social capital, and other resources to explore two religious traditions deeply and publicly.[13] Elite practitioners are usually academics or religious leaders, some of whom even earn tenure on university faculties by researching and writing about religious multiplicity. Unfortunately, most of their scholarship is unavailable to the general reader; instead, it is written for specialists and published in expensive journals with limited circulation. (A significant exception is Paul Knitter's *New York Times* best seller, *Without Buddha I Could Not Be a Christian*.)

Even if more people had access to this literature, however, I suspect the audience would still be limited. People curious about, living with, or exploring spiritual fluidity are not always concerned about religious multiplicity as a doctrinal issue, a cognitive choice, or an academic subject. They want to understand what it's like to live spiritually fluid lives: How do people come to claim (and be claimed by) multiple spiritual and religious traditions? How do they navigate the tensions and possibilities inherent to maintaining bonds with multiple religions? Can spiritually fluid people reconcile conflicting beliefs, or do they even care about the contradictions? These questions are especially germane under certain circumstances. The questions matter when religious multiplicity is structural—that is, when spiritually fluid people inherit multiple religions from their families (as when a child's parents come from different religious traditions). And the questions especially apply when multiplicity has been imposed through colonialism or other social and economic realities (as when Jews in fourteenth-century Spain publicly converted to Catholicism to avoid punishment by the Inquisition but secretly remained Jewish, celebrating Shabbat and other rituals behind closed doors).[14]

THE RISKS OF RELIGIOUS MULTIPLICITY

The risks of engaging in exceptional spirituality—implicit and explicit, real and perceived—can be seen among Spanish Muslims and Jews during the Inquisition (a church effort to find and suppress heresies). In medieval Spain and Portugal, conversion to Catholicism did not protect *conversos* and *Moriscos* from violence; their Christian orthodoxy was tightly monitored for traces of Islam and Judaism, and they took great pains to avoid any appearance of religious multiplicity, even as many of them continued practicing their original religions in secret while publicly performing a Christian identity.

I relate to this, in some ways. I didn't face an inquisition when I was discerning ordination to Christian ministry, but the risks of violating institutional expectations became clear during my first meeting with the committee that would shepherd me through the process.

In the Presbyterian Church (USA), discernment begins with "inquirers" telling the story of their faith journeys to a committee of local people who represent the denomination. When I entered the room and told my story, I naively presented the Buddhist training and practice I had experienced as a gift for ministry, something to be welcomed by the church. Then I waited for the committee's questions. The committee members didn't ask about gifts for ministry. They didn't initially ask how Buddhism had shaped me or how my personal journey could create strengths and resources for professional service. They wanted to know if my spirituality was normal, in the sense described above. One of the first questions came from an older Korean American pastor in a suit and tie.

"Mr. Bidwell, do you believe that Jesus Christ is the only way to achieve salvation and spend eternity in heaven with God?"

I didn't—and don't—think salvation is a human achievement or that we spend eternity with God in a location called *heaven*. I knew the "right" answer to his question, from his perspective, but I didn't know what the committee as a whole would accept. I was silent for a long time. My face flushed. Answering honestly risked putting my professional future at stake, as if I were kneeling before a sovereign ruler who would judge whether I was worthy to enter the kingdom.

The pastor repeated his question: "Do you believe that Jesus Christ is the only way to achieve salvation and spend eternity in heaven with God?"

"No," I said. "I don't believe that."

We sat in silence until he said, "Mr. Bidwell. Have you heard the phrase 'I am the Way and the Truth and the Life; no one comes to the Father except through me'?"

I nodded. "Of course," I said. "But remember that Jesus in the Gospel of John is speaking as the Logos, the ruling principle of the universe, a concept Christians adopted from Hellenistic philosophy. And we don't know that Jesus ever said those words; the writers of John had their own purposes for including them. Those words have a context we have to consider."

I should have stopped with "of course."

The pastor slammed shut the binder that held my written materials. "In Korea," he said, "we have a saying: You judge a tree by its first leaf. I think I've seen yours."

The Christian Bible, of course, encourages us to judge a tree by its fruit, not its first leaf—but it didn't seem wise to point that out. So I sat in silence until the committee chair changed the subject.

In the end, the committee approved me as an inquirer to the ordination process, the first step in a two-year progression that would involve several votes. Afterward, the committee chair told me, "You're a new animal, something we haven't encountered before—the first of many, I suspect. And the committee doesn't quite know what to do with these changes." I must have looked concerned, because she quickly added, "What happened today doesn't mean you don't have a call to ordained ministry. But it might not be a call to *Presbyterian* ministry. That's what the process will discern."

What happened during that meeting? On the one hand, the process was appropriate: the church was discerning whether I could faithfully represent its identity, doctrine, and authority as an ordained leader. On the other hand, the conversation was a confluence of power, culture, authority, interpretation, and expectations that determine what's "normal." I walked away with the unspoken assessment that my spiritual identity was dangerous, a threat to the institutional church and therefore a liability to me and to the denomination. From that point, without making a conscious decision, I kept religious multiplicity in the background of the ordination process. Instead of an identity, Buddhist-Christian studies became an academic interest, an area of critical scholarship. I buried its autobiographical dimensions until I had been ordained, completed a PhD, and decided to serve in higher education instead of congregational ministry. In most situations, I passed as a singular Christian.

I am not the only Christian clergyperson to experience the church's erasure or rejection of spiritual fluidity. In 2009, Episcopal priest Ann Holmes Redding was defrocked for identifying "100 percent" as both Christian and Muslim. She said she belonged to both in the same way that she is both black and a woman. She sees the traditions as siblings, related but different. When she was disciplined by the church, her bishops issued a statement: "A priest of the Church cannot be both a Christian and a Muslim."[15] Later the same year, a regional body of the Episcopal Church elected a bishop described as "walking the path of Christianity and Zen Buddhism together." His election was nullified by the national church and a majority of its bishops.[16]

Decisions like the rejection of the priest and the bishop—and other decisions more damaging, even life-threatening—happen because spiritual monogamy has been a norm in North Atlantic cultures for most of the medieval and modern eras. We consider it healthy, appropriate, and even necessary to link ourselves to a particular religious tradition, even at the risk of persecution or death (not to mention the threat of eternal damnation). Throughout history, religious identity and affiliation have carried compelling social, political, and economic consequences; they still do today. Consider the risks involved with singular religious identities in some situations, then ponder how much riskier multiplicity would be.[17]

There are historical records, for example, that show political and spiritual leaders ostracizing Buddhists, damning Jews, rallying Crusaders to rout Muslims from the Holy Land, bombing Christian churches, privileging Hindus over Sikhs, and separating "pagan" children from parents in the name of Jesus. When the Roman Empire became the Holy Roman Empire (by making

Christianity its official religion), it encouraged conversion by giving legal and economic privileges to Christians. Likewise, Christians in British and French colonies such as Ceylon and Indochina received better jobs than did Hindus, Buddhists, Muslims, and practitioners of other religions. In mid-twentieth-century Vietnam, Catholics persecuted Buddhists and followers of Cao Dai; today in Sri Lanka, Buddhists battle Muslims and persecute Christians. Violence among Hindus, Muslims, and Sikhs partly defined twentieth-century India. In Iraq, Sunni Muslims receive death threats in Shia neighborhoods. In China and elsewhere, Jehovah's Witnesses, Catholic bishops, Protestant Christians, and other religious people are imprisoned. Christian peace workers in Iraq and the Democratic Republic of the Congo are tortured and executed. The US war on terror has, depending on your perspective, overt or thinly disguised religious overtones. In Indonesia, marriage across religious lines is forbidden, and similar legislation has been on the table in Myanmar. All over the world, families disown and disinherit children and grandchildren who leave the family faith, marry someone from another tradition, or explore spiritual alternatives.

Religious identity and affiliation matter, especially when religious singularity is the norm. Normal spirituality requires clear boundaries: you are in or you are out. Blurring religious lines is not an option; families and institutions expect, demand, and privilege singular spiritual-religious identities. People judge what you think, say, and do against the teachings of one faith, and you're expected to defend and preserve your tradition. Some people with singular religious identities find their "truth" worth dying for.

This account is too simple, of course; I've conveniently created a binary between multiplicity and singularity because it serves my purposes. In fact, even single, discrete religious traditions (or what we perceive as single, discrete traditions) are multiple. Religious and spiritual traditions have always borrowed freely from each other, usually without formal acknowledgment. Prayer beads—commonly known as rosaries—were original to Buddhism, transmitted to Islam, then adopted by Christians during the Crusades.[18] Christians adopted and adapted Jewish texts. Muslims bow in prayer in part because Christians did, and Christians bowed in prayer in part because Jews did, and Jews stopped bowing in prayer to distinguish themselves from other Abrahamic faiths. As Buddhism, initially a reform of Hindu thought and practice, moved east into China, Japan and Korea and north into Tibet, it incorporated Confucian, Taoist, and Bon philosophies and senses of spirituality. Thomas Merton's description of *le point vierge*, the still, small spark at the center of humans that belongs entirely to God, has inspired Christians for decades—but the Catholic monk and mystic borrowed the idea from a medieval Muslim mystic without identifying its source.

What's more, singular identities sometimes mask multiple practices: As described earlier, Jewish families in Spain and Portugal converted to Catholicism to save themselves from the Inquisition but continued Shabbat rituals in secret, and Buddhists in Sri Lanka (then known as Ceylon) converted to Christianity to qualify for stable, higher-paying jobs but still participated in ceremonies at Buddhist and Hindu temples. In North and South America, governments insisted that indigenous nations "civilize" themselves by becoming Christian, a policy that made indigenous people hide their spirituality beneath a veneer of church language and practice. (Don't assume we've stopped erasing First Nations religion: "The problem with Indian Presbyterians," one denominational executive said to me more than a decade ago, "is that they want to be Indian and Presbyterian at the same time.")

Outside the North Atlantic region, religious lines aren't always so sharp. European missionaries encountered this porosity as they began to evangelize people in various regions of Asia.

When Catholic priests arrived in India, for example, the emperor Akbar delighted the Jesuits who came to convert him. He assured them that he had indeed become a Christian—and then infuriated them by continuing to worship as a Muslim and, in many ways, a Hindu. This multiplicity was not what the Jesuits had in mind at all and is yet another incident that reveals how Europeans regarded the boundaries between religions as impregnable, whereas Indians saw the lines as rather porous.[19]

In Asia, people pray at Taoist altars, Buddhist temples, and Christian churches, all on the same day. Sufi Muslims in Kashmir and elsewhere turn to the nondualism of Hinduism and Buddhism to deepen their appreciation of Islam. Aztec and Mayan people in Mexico and South America adopted the forms of Catholicism but continued to worship indigenous deities-in-disguise, who were clothed in the regalia of Christian saints. In Africa, followers of Chrislam worship both Jesus and Allah, and the Garifuna people of Belize and other parts of coastal Central America practice a type of shamanism that incorporates ancestor worship, spirit worship, and Catholic doctrine and rituals. In the United States and Canada, cultural Jews practice Buddhist mindfulness while worshipping at the synagogue.[20] And in Mexico, at least one Catholic woman has a Hindu soul.

COMPLEX RELIGIOUS BONDS, CULTURAL APPROPRIATION, AND WHITE PRIVILEGE

Sometimes what passes as religious multiplicity becomes cultural appropriation.[21] Taking bits and pieces of a religion for personal use—even for sincere reasons—can do violence to the tradition and to people for whom the tradition is a family, cultural, and social identity. This practice becomes especially problematic when white people from developed nations turn to religious imagery, vocabulary, dress, and behavior from minority communities in attempts to appear exotic or radical, to claim superior spiritual understanding, or to make a fashion statement. Simply put, appropriation is a form of colonization: "Colonial powers not only extracted natural resources," writes law professor Olufunmilayo Arewa, "but also cultural booty."[22] Religion and spirituality can be a form of cultural booty, especially when divorced from the cultures and structures that sustain it in its historical settings.

When does religious borrowing become appropriation, exploitation, or an unethical expression of privilege? This question, serious and important, isn't simple. The line between borrowing and appropriation varies from context to context and remains too nebulous to address sufficiently in this book. Religious boundaries are always shifting. So are cultural, linguistic, and artistic boundaries. Borrowing across religious traditions has been a norm whenever and wherever different communities encounter one another, and these exchanges have benefited human spirituality around the world.

For me, borrowing becomes appropriation when it exploits people and communities. First, a person (or community) with significant cultural power and privilege—in the form of money, status, influence, recognition, and other forms of capital—takes or adopts a resource from marginalized people and communities. Then the person or community uses that resource to consolidate or gain more power and privilege. Think about Apple, for example, when it used a portrait of the Dalai Lama to sell computers—even with his prior permission. Exploitation of this type is especially heinous when the appropriator claims credit for a spiritual practice or identifies it as a human truth that belongs to everyone without acknowledging or valuing its particular cultural origins, history, community norms, and purposes.

Few spiritually fluid people I meet, however, appropriate or exploit traditions. Their economic and cultural privilege sometimes makes multiplicity possible in terms of having resources to study, learn, travel, and engage in more than one tradition, but they have authentic commitments and bonds to those traditions. The longevity of a person's multiple bonds and the depth of practice as measured against each tradition's criteria for growth are ways to distinguish religious borrowing from religious appropriation.

RELIGIOUS MULTIPLICITY
AND HUMAN FLOURISHING

Spiritually fluid people tell a lot of stories about living with multiplicity. One man remembers his encounter with the health-care system.

Before dawn, in a dim hospital lobby, Jeffrey sat in front of an admitting nurse prior to a routine outpatient surgery. The nurse read brusquely from a computer screen, and Jeffrey murmured a sleepy response to each question. The nurse seemed bored; clearly, she repeated each question hundreds of times a week.

"Religious preference?" she said.

Jeffrey smiled. "Part of me is Tibetan Buddhist," he said, "and part of me is Catholic."

The nurse looked at him for the first time. "Which part is having surgery today?" she asked.

"Both."

The nurse peered over her glasses. "Sir, the form only allows you to have one religious preference. Will it be 'Buddhist' or 'Catholic Christian'?"

"I'm both," Jeffrey repeated.

"I'll just check 'Other,'" she said. "Unless you prefer 'None.'"

Jeffrey didn't respond, and the nurse moved to the next question. After surgery, he learned that his official hospital record read "No Religious Affiliation."

On the one hand, this notation was no big deal. Jeffrey did not suffer materially because of the misidentification. If something had gone badly, the nurse's action might have complicated the work of the hospital chaplains, and staff might have had more difficulty contacting Jeffrey's congregations or religious leaders. But the surgery had gone well. Jeffrey's suffering was existential, psychosocial, and deeply personal: the hospital had silenced his sense of the sacred and denied his religion because he didn't fit into the official categories.

"She erased my spirituality," he says. "My spirituality is important to me, and I wasn't allowed to claim it. I was having surgery, and my religion should have been offering comfort; it should have been a resource for coping. Instead I felt as if I needed to defend it. I felt like I wasn't legitimately 'spiritual.' Would it be that hard to change the computer program so people can choose two or more religions if that's who they are?"

Scholars consider events like these micro-aggressions. Micro-aggressions function as social shrapnel—tiny, almost invisible slights against someone's personhood. These verbal and behavioral cuts grind people down, keep them on the margin, and communicate their lack of value to the dominant culture. They prevent people from flourishing.

This book's broad inquiry—how a person can claim or be claimed by two religions simultaneously—is a key question for human meaning and flourishing in the twenty-first century. Our responses to spiritual fluidity shape social norms, family life, education, religious institutions, public policy, and professional practice. How, for example, will hospitals, schools, and the US Census account for people whose religious preference or affiliation doesn't fit neatly into one box? Can a Chindu employee—someone who is simultaneously Hindu and Christian—take paid time off for both Holi and Christmas? In Indonesia, where the government requires each person to declare a single religious affiliation, can someone who officially identifies as Muslim but practices *vipassana* meditation and studies at a temple receive a scholarship for students in the dharma traditions? Should an interfaith child—progeny of a Jewish mother and Christian father—receive baptism, a bar/bat mitzvah, or both? How do we discern whether someone is committed to two (or more) traditions or is just religi-curious?[23]

Religious multiplicity isn't a fad or a tiny movement. Its increasing visibility challenges the illusion of singular religious identities and the expectation of lifelong fidelity to one spiritual tradition. As mentioned earlier, the nearly one-third of US adults attending religious services outside their tradition were doing so not because of an interfaith marriage. People in mixed-faith relationships are no more (and no less) likely than the rest of the public to worship in multiple religious traditions. Research in Australia suggests that dual religious belonging—a particular form of religious multiplicity—does exist in varying degrees on cognitive, emotional, and behavioral levels. In fact, talking with religiously multiple people convinced the researcher to conclude: "Dual (or multi-) religious belonging . . . is not only possible but desirable."[24] After careful critical study, British theologian Rose Drew concluded that Buddhist-Christian identity and practice can be logical and consistent and do not need to compromise the tenets of either tradition.

From my perspective, most people of faith are spiritually fluid to one degree or another; they commit to one religion in name but incorporate many religions in practice. Some do so formally; for example, the Maria Kannon Zen Center in Dallas intentionally includes Buddhists, Christians, and Buddhist-Christians. The Oriental Orthodox Order in the West identifies itself as a Christian tradition that draws on Islam, Buddhism, First Nations spirituality, and other traditions. Osage Forest of Peace in Oklahoma started as a Hindu-Christian ashram staffed by Benedictine nuns; now it is an interfaith, interspiritual retreat center. The architecture of an Anglican church in Iran includes the opening words of the Qur'an written in Arabic to form a cross: *In the name of God, the Merciful, the Compassionate One.* In 2014, 2015, and 2016, the World Council of Churches and the United Church of Christ held meetings in India and the United States to discern pastoral responses to religious multiplicity.

CREATING NEW WAYS OF TALKING
ABOUT RELIGIOUS MULTIPLICITY

Because of spiritually fluid people like Fidelia, Jeffrey, and thousands like them, we need new ways of talking about religious and spiritual identity. It's no longer sufficient (if it ever was) to assign a singular, monolithic label to a person's beliefs and expect the person to behave accordingly, as if it's easy to tell who's inside or outside, who's a true believer and who's not. Ordinary people who live religiously multiple lives are seldom celebrated and often unseen. They hide their multiple allegiances from family members who will not tolerate someone practicing a different faith; they mask themselves in one or more of their religious communities to avoid shame, judgment, punishment, or other negative consequences; and they switch from one type of religious language to another, depending on context. They celebrate only one set of religious holidays in the workplace. Frequently, they pass as Christians because doing so bestows cultural and religious privilege.

Most religiously multiple people in the United States engage in their spirituality quietly, experiencing various seasons as their multiplicity shifts and changes: curiosity about multiple traditions; engagement through serious study and practice; ripening as their understanding become more sophisticated and they experience greater comfort with complex religious bonds; and generativity, in which they largely move beyond suffering caused by complex religious bonds and mentor others who are on spiritually fluid paths. Few friends, family members, or coworkers know about their complicated religious bonds, and their spiritual fluidity is mostly unseen or pushed to the margins of their identities, their communities, and their public religious behavior. This marginalization, and the stigma that piles up on those who honor multiple religious bonds, can be painful, isolating people from their communities and their families, awakening shame, and creating the type of self-surveillance that guards against accidently revealing what you really believe, who you really worship, and how you really practice. Yet religious multiplicity also has tremendous gifts for religious communities, civil life, and intimate relationships.

When we listen to spiritually fluid people and their experiences, we expand their freedom to engage in and share their spiritual experiences. In this book, I am primarily accountable to spiritually fluid people and only secondarily to religious communities, institutions, doctrines, intellectual traditions like logic and psychology, and ideas about "normality." By providing a conceptual map of the pathways to religious multiplicity—and suggesting a shared language for talking about its realities—I want to shift how religious leaders, family members, cultural institutions, and people with singular religious identities relate to spiritually fluid people.

Three questions shape the story that follows:

- In a world that privileges singular religious identities, how do spiritually fluid people come to claim and be claimed by multiple religious bonds?

- What allows spiritually fluid people to navigate possibly conflicting beliefs and participate in multiple religions?

- How do spiritually fluid beliefs and practices help people and communities flourish?

My response describes three pathways—choice, inheritance, and collaboration. These pathways allow people to shape seemingly contradictory beliefs into coherent identities, life-giving practices, and deeply transformative spiritual lives—spiritual lives that have integrity and disclose truth.

CHAPTER TWO

Choosing

Sometimes it takes a crisis to turn people toward God. That's what happened to Marie Romo. She grew up with the implicit rules of her Mexican American community: first, girls should be seen, not heard, and second, girls find security in marriage and motherhood. But these rules failed her by the time she was twenty. Her husband's abuse offered no security, as documented by her bruises and self-doubt, and keeping quiet hadn't made things better. After the divorce, Marie became a single mom with three children and no driver's license, no diploma, no job, no work history, and no prospects. "I didn't know who or what I could count on," she remembers. "It was just me and the kids, and I certainly couldn't count on myself."

Out of instinct, she turned to God. Although her parents and siblings aren't religious, Marie was baptized as an infant (baptism is a Christian sacrament marking formal entry into the universal church), and growing up, she absorbed the popular piety of the local Hispanic Catholic community. "I just said, 'OK, God, it's all up to you now,'" she remembers. "I had nothing else but to surrender to him. I thought, 'No matter what, I put everything—these kids, everything—up to you.' . . . I just prayed and prayed and prayed. And my girls were going, 'What are you doing?' I told them . . . , 'I'm asking for guidance because I have no idea what we are going to do.'"

Years later, faced with another crisis—a terminal diagnosis

36

for a lung condition—Marie experimented with yogic breathing to improve her health. This practice led to voracious reading of Hindu philosophy. Before long, she was studying Hindu teachings with a swami while remaining tied to Christianity. Twenty years later, Marie still practices Hinduism, still honors God, still studies religion, and is still alive. She credits her spirituality. At fifty-seven years old, she now teaches Hindu concepts to others. Her family and community call her *doña*, a respectful title for a wise and experienced woman. Yes, they're sometimes scandalized to learn that their *doña* prays to the Christian God *and* engages in Hindu practices, but those practices are Marie's spiritual touchstones.

"Hinduism for me is a workshop, a tool," she says. "Everybody sees the guru: 'Oh, he's your God.' No. He's a tool that keeps me grounded and closer to God. . . . If you have that [initial] connection with God, Hinduism connects you to yourself and to God even closer. I don't look at swami as my God. I see him as a tool, an instructor to get me closer to God." Today she occasionally attends Christian worship, practices Vedic breathing daily, reads the Bible, studies the Upanishads, takes frequent solitary retreats, and teaches Hindu meditation to her granddaughter and others.

Like many spiritually fluid people, Marie came to religious multiplicity not because of doctrine but because it seemed useful to adopt the practices of a second tradition.

"Like reading scripture," Marie says. "Sometimes, reading something will go: 'Wow! I connect with this!' Take that. Take the scripture that's really talking to you right now and feel it, read it, absorb it—because that's God that's talking to you. Not the book, not the people, but God is showing you his word, his message. And it's beautiful. . . . I believe anywhere I go, God is my guide. I'll just say, 'I don't know what I'm doing, let's go!'— because I don't."

Like Marie, some people *choose* multiplicity as a spiritual path.[1] They are not born into it, they don't receive it from their culture, yet they decide to make it a part of their lives. The path usually starts with curiosity: they encounter an unfamiliar religion, explore its ideas and practices, and eventually begin to correlate its beliefs and practices with the spiritual tradition where they originally made their home. For some, the process appears largely cognitive. Scholars and religious professionals seeking coherence in multiplicity, for example, describe themselves as crossing from one set of metaphysics, ontologies, and truth claims to another, then returning to their home traditions. Some seek to reconcile the traditions; others simply look for intersections, ideas, and practices that are compatible.

But who typically chooses religious multiplicity? And how did it become an option?

WHO CHOOSES MULTIPLICITY?

This chapter focuses on those we might call spiritual nomads, people who consciously ignore boundaries between religious territories to find shelter, nourishment, and meaning in fertile landscapes, familiar or not. In some ways, these nomads are like indigenous people around the world, honoring geographies rather than legal and political boundaries. They know where they belong, no matter what borders cross their territory. Nomads belong to a particular landscape, not a particular nation-state; they go where they find life, even if it means ignoring borders drawn by others. Likewise, spiritually fluid people accept that a religious boundary doesn't necessarily mark a sharp transition between cultures, beliefs, or landscapes: in terms of topography and culture, one side of the Rio Grande is pretty much like the other. Their spiritual territories straddle institutional and doctrinal lines. They don't cross borders so much as borders cross them, segmenting a holistic experience into separate parts with different labels.

In general, three types of people choose religious multiplicity.[2] There are those born into and committed to one religious tradition but attracted to another for a variety of reasons. Second, some people convert from one religion to another (or descend from converts) and begin to explore and appreciate what was lost when they left their original religious traditions. Finally, some religiously multiple people see value in several religious traditions but might not identify fully with any. This group includes many influenced by migration, international travel, and mass communication, such as religious "nones" (people who explore various spiritual beliefs and practices but who don't, or won't, align with a formal religious tradition or community) and people who say they are spiritual but not religious (SBNR). Among Christians, changes to church doctrine—especially Pope Paul VI's 1965 declaration *Nostra Aetate*, which encouraged relationships with other religions—helped make religious multiplicity possible.

The church's new openness, for example, created conditions that allowed Ruben Habito to claim a Buddhist-Christian identity—or as he put it to me, to identify as "a Zen Buddhist practicing as a Roman Catholic Christian." In 1970, Ruben was a Jesuit in the Philippines, preparing for Catholic ordination. In light of *Nostra Aetate*, the church had sent him to Japan as a missionary, asking him to learn about the Japanese Buddhist tradition to help the church understand what God had given to the world through Buddhism. In addition to formal classroom study, Ruben learned experientially through Zen practice. "In the beginning," Ruben told me,

> it was simply a way of sitting and breathing and being aware. So it was a form of spirituality informed by the Buddhist tradition that I had started as a Christian, with the confidence that it would confirm and enhance, and also deepen, my own Christian understanding. . . . I found a certain affinity or a sense of attraction that drew me more and more to it. And I found myself gradually

identifying with it in a sense that it's a worldview that represents phenomena with a certain understanding that somehow connects and somehow makes sense. And it made sense to me.

An interior dialogue ensued as Ruben brought Catholic doctrine, Buddhist practice, Buddhist doctrine, and his formation as a priest into conversation to "see whether they could be together, whether they could be taken in, in a way that did not contradict one or the other."

During our conversation, Ruben recited the Apostle's Creed, one of the Christian church's earliest affirmations, and said, "I have to ask myself, 'What do I mean when I say those things?' And somehow it needed to be sorted out in a way that did not contradict what I was already experiencing when I sat [in meditation] as a Zen Buddhist."

For Ruben, it was meditation practice—zazen—that allowed the traditions to come together without contradicting each other. "It had nothing to do with conceptual formulations," he remembers. "It was something that was challenging me and inviting me to launch deeper and deeper into a deeper level. . . . One affirmation was that I didn't even have to be Buddhist or Christian to be able to really partake of the fruits of Zen."

Eventually, Ruben left the Jesuit order and Catholic priesthood. He remained a Catholic lay leader and was ordained as a teacher in the Sanbo Kyodan lineage of Japanese Zen. Today he teaches spirituality and world religions at Perkins School of Theology, a Christian seminary in Dallas. He is a noted scholar of Buddhist-Christian studies and the founding teacher of the Maria Kannon Zen Center in Dallas, a meditation center named after Mary, the mother of Jesus, and Kannon, the Buddhist bodhisattva of compassion. He describes the two traditions as "mutually enriching . . . the same, but not the same."

If Ruben represents a sort of strong multiplicity—identifying and participating in two traditions as sources of truth—other spiritually fluid people maintain softer or weaker bonds to multiple traditions.[3] This soft multiplicity often occurs among the SBNRs and religious nones.[4] Some people who consider themselves spiritually fluid choose "none" on surveys and institutional forms that require them to choose a single religious identity. Marie, for example, considers herself a religious none; even though she's shaped by Christianity and Hinduism, she says she can fit into any religious community. "I respect everything," she says. "I respect it, and I take tools to help me grow."

Research suggests that people in these categories emphasize individual spiritual authority, pragmatism, and connection both to creation and to other people as an aspect of spirituality. They see spirituality as immanent, rooted in the concrete here and now, rather than transcendent, oriented toward a world beyond this one. Spiritual freedom becomes a central value; they walk the pathway of choice to construct idiosyncratic forms of spirituality from bits and pieces of religious wisdom. Few establish deep roots in any tradition. Even without engaging particular traditions with depth or rigor, however, they often articulate clear beliefs (especially about religious authority and the nature of the ultimate) and share consistent spiritual practices with others.

These shared beliefs and practices suggest a shift from collective religion to private, individual religion, according to theologian Linda Mercadante. "Since [SBNRs] have been deprived of ascribed roles and inherited meaning," she writes, "they have had no choice but to try to make meaning with the bits and pieces they find lying around."[5] The meaning they construct might be private, but it is remarkably consistent: SBNRs reject religious exclusivism, dogmatism, judgment, and the concept of sin; advocate internal spiritual authority; make pragmatic and therapeutic use of spiritual practices to achieve liberation; and see nature as a source or mediator of spirituality. They have a strong commitment to a universal truth that underlies all religions, and they see internal happiness and peace as the ultimate goals of spirituality.

The practices of SBNRs and religious nones, however, make their spirituality seem less private and individual. Most of their practices fall under what religion scholar Elizabeth Drescher calls the four *F*s of contemporary spirituality: family, friends, food (shared meals and gatherings), and Fido (spending time in nature with pets).[6] Embedded in everyday life, these practices center on relationships and integrate body, mind, and spirit. They allow religious nones to share stories, generate conversation, and encourage common action—activities more important to them than religious affiliation or shared belief.

"To claim 'None' as the label for one's spiritual identity," Drescher says,

> is to refuse to participate in the normative system of religious identification, where labels suggest general agreement with beliefs, values, and practices that distinguish one religious institution from another. . . . Given this, labeling one's own spiritual identity as outside institutional religion is both to resist a long-standing cultural insistence on at least the pretense of religious affiliation and to identify as an outsider, an other—an "un"—within the normative religious culture.[7]

Religious identification, then, becomes a spiritual practice in and of itself, and claiming "none" allows people to strategically hide or reveal religious perspectives and practices in different relationships and social settings.

"Claiming the label 'None,'" Drescher writes, "does not mean that a person sees herself as 'nothing' spiritually, but that she elects not to describe her spirituality either in institutional religious terms or fraught categories like Atheist or Agnostic. 'I'm none of *that*,' she is saying, even when much of 'that' may factor into her own spirituality and the story it allows her to tell about who she is in the world."[8]

Spiritual practices for Drescher go far beyond those associated with particular religious traditions; they are "a dynamic blend of actions, attitudes, preferences, material objects, feelings, and thoughts that forms coherent ways of living with others in the world."[9] Seen this way, she argues, today's spiritual practices suggest that "more diversely resourced, everyday spiritualities are becoming the norm,"[10] with being and becoming more important than believing, belonging, and behaving. For religious nones, spirituality emerges "organically from the whole of life in relation to a diversity of others, rather [than] being structured through categories of propositional beliefs, affiliational patterns, and the associated ritual and social actions of defined religious groups."[11]

HOW DID MULTIPLICITY BECOME A CHOICE?

This turn toward religious choice, the embrace of fluid spirituality in which being and becoming are more valuable than doctrine and belonging, didn't happen on a whim. It gradually emerged in response to social and historical circumstances that support multiplicity. Some of these circumstances are recent; others, centuries old. Simply put, politics and economics shape complex religious bonds. Expanded US immigration policy, for example, seems to be the biggest influence on the choice of religious multiplicity in the United States. During and after the 1960s, new immigration policies increased religious diversity in the United States, exposing religious leaders and laity alike to neighbors and colleagues who claimed Buddhism, Candomblé, Hinduism, Santeria, Sikhism, Islam, Taoism, Umbanda, and Vodun as religious homes. At the same time, cultural values became more open to different values, cultures, and religious expressions.[12]

The Second Vatican Council (1962–1965) of the Catholic

Church contributed to this shift as well. In the 1965 document *Nostra Aetate*, the Catholic hierarchy "declared a positive regard for the religions of humankind," writes Taoist Christian scholar John Berthrong.[13] The document presents the world's religions as God's gifts to humanity and encourages Catholic Christians—like Ruben Habito—to engage with other religions to the extent that these faiths reflect church teaching. Suddenly, people not only had access to multiple religions but also had the church's blessing to engage with them in meaningful ways.

Today's complex religious belonging also reflects centuries of Christian expansion beyond Europe. Through encounters with local spiritualities and other religious traditions, Christian missionaries have seen spiritual fluidity as an option for centuries. Those sympathetic to local religions, like Ruben, sometimes developed spiritually fluid ideas, practices, and identities. At the same time, local residents forced or persuaded to convert to Christianity might continue to practice their original religions in secret. Other local people converted (or added Christianity to their mix of spiritualities) because of the link between Christianity, social mobility, and economic privilege. By adopting *strategic multiplicity*—performing Christian norms in public while practicing original traditions at home—local people gained access to otherwise unattainable economic and social goods. In nineteenth-century Ceylon (now Sri Lanka), for example, Christian baptism was a prerequisite for a government job. "Many, therefore, had gone through this formality and attended Christian worship," Elisabeth J. Harris writes. "But they had not thereby stopped going to their Buddhist or Hindu temples, and the Dutch authorities turned a blind eye, more concerned about trading profits than enforcing exclusivist patterns of religious belonging."[14]

While being spiritually fluid could literally save the lives of colonized people, others benefited primarily by becoming monoreligious Christians. Today, the descendants of colonized people are returning to their spiritual ancestry by incorporating it into Christianity: African American Christians and African American Muslims incorporate Yoruba, Dinka traditions, Ifá, and Candomblé into their spiritualities, while Filipino Christians adopt and adapt the traditional babaylan practices suppressed by Spanish colonizers.[15] The lingering influence of the Christian colonial project, then, still shapes the people's choices to develop and sustain complex religious bonds.

Much of the historical literature about spiritual fluidity comes from colonizers—especially missionaries—who developed complex religious bonds.[16] When missionaries traveled great distances to bring Christianity to people, the local people exposed the missionaries to a variety of philosophies, forms of spirituality, and religious traditions. Living in the midst of unfamiliar languages and customs, missionaries adapted Christianity to local settings by presenting church teaching in forms familiar to the local population. There is evidence, for example, that Eastern Orthodox missionaries in western China adopted the form and imagery of Taoist texts to teach about the "Religion of Light," the name they chose to describe Christianity. These missionaries emphasized how Christianity was consistent with familiar Taoist, Confucian, and Buddhist teachings.[17]

This acculturation required missionaries to gain intimate knowledge of other religions. Some missionaries developed great respect and even sympathy for the teachings and practices of those traditions. In addition, close friendships with non-Christian people led some missionaries to accept and value other religious traditions; they could no longer believe that a loving God would condemn non-Christians.

Pioneers included the French Benedictine monk Dom Henri Le Saux, who moved to India early in the twentieth century to search for a simpler life. Eventually, he adopted the Hindu practice of *sannyasa* (renunciation), forming a Hindu-Christian ashram and taking the Hindu name Swami Abhishiktananda. "He had a Christian experience," writes religion scholar Michael

Amaladoss. "He had a Hindu one. But they were not different. They were not the same, either. They were non-two, advaitic. The double identity does not disappear, but becomes a communion."[18] Abhishiktananda's friend Bede Griffiths, a British Benedictine monk, also lived in Christian-Hindu ashrams in India and took the Hindu name Swami Dayananda late in life.

In Japan, the German Jesuit Hugo M. Enomiya-Lassalle explored Zen spirituality and later was ordained as a Zen *roshi* (teacher) while remaining a Catholic priest.[19] In Sri Lanka, Catholic priest Michael Rodrigo infused Christian ministry with Buddhist understandings of liberation and founded the Christian-Buddhist Dialogue Center in Colombo. The Jesuit priest and missionary Aloysius Pieris holds two doctorates, one in Christian theology and one in Buddhist studies. With the support of the Catholic Church, he founded a Christian ashramic community in Sri Lanka; the community has become a primary site for lived explorations of complex religious bonds.[20]

Missionaries and scholars who claim complex religious bonds usually value religious community, grant authority to historical religious and spiritual traditions, and sometimes hold institutional power as religious leaders in one or more communities. These values set them apart from the SBNRs and religious nones—both of which are becoming prominent today in the United States and Europe.

RELIGIOUS BORDERLANDS
AND THE NATURE OF CHOICE

It's clear, then, that shifting boundaries—geographical, existential, sociopolitical, and theological—attract many to religious borderlands, places where spiritual beliefs, customs, languages, and relationships mingle.[21] Sometimes, these explorers claim dual religious citizenship. For many (but not all) of them, complex religious bonds represent an intellectual and a volitional process that never ends, but matures and becomes more sophisticated over time. Marie, for example, began to explore Hinduism when she was faced with her own death; at first, Hinduism was an unfamiliar religion that spoke to her physical and existential needs. Finding this religion increasingly meaningful, useful, and provocative, she began to correlate Hindu beliefs and practices with the religion of her spiritual homeland in Hispanic Catholicism.

Marie doesn't especially seek or value intellectual or doctrinal coherence in her spiritual life, but many spiritually fluid people do. They work diligently to reconcile different claims of truth, views of the world, and visions of the ultimate; when people fail at reconciliation, they seek ways to hold the differences in tension without rejecting what they value in various traditions. Some seekers, such as religion scholar Catherine Cornille, argue that all religions share a fundamental ultimate reality but express it differently, whereas others, such as theologian Mark Heim, think that different traditions reflect distinct and equally valid ends—that is, different types of salvation—while affirming one as more desirable than another.[22] Some people ignore questions about religious ends and instead interpret the symbols and teachings of one tradition through the lens of another. They see traditions as complementary, able to scrutinize each other and thus construct fuller understandings of truth.

Among religious leaders, scholars, and others who approach religion from largely analytic, critical, and rational perspectives, intellectual motives often seem primary. People following this cognitive pathway to multiplicity seek to examine each tradition to develop a fuller and more sympathetic understanding of each religion and a clearer appreciation of the various religions' similarities and differences.

Most who choose multiplicity begin by emphasizing the similarities between traditions; only later do contradictions become important. This dynamic shaped my complex religious bonds. When I began to learn Christian theology after years of Buddhist study and practice, I looked for simple correspondences between the two doctrinal approaches. My notes contain statements like "Christian sin = Buddhist ignorance" and "Christian *agape* (love) corresponds to Buddhist *metta* (loving-kindness)." Only later did I realize that Christian love and Buddhist loving-kindness have different foundations and emphases. If I want to equate sin with ignorance, as I did so facilely in my notes, I need to significantly adjust my understanding of both concepts. The shift from similarities and correspondences to differences and contradictions reflects the psychological processes of assimilation and accommodation proposed by Swiss developmental psychologist Jean Piaget.

Accommodation and assimilation work like this: When people learn about a new religious tradition, they tend first to assimilate its teachings into their spiritual-religious understanding from the past, fitting the new tradition into the categories of the old. For example, the idea of nirvana/Buddhist liberation might be placed into a mental file titled "Heaven/Christian salvation," as if the two concepts are closely aligned. Only later, as people explore more fully and with greater nuance, do they accommodate new traditions by making changes to their existing religious ideas—realizing that nirvana needs its own folder because it's not a subset of, or equivalent to, heaven.

Paul Knitter, a theologian and former Catholic priest, demonstrates the cognitive pathway to complex religious bonds. Knitter moved long ago from assimilation to accommodation; rather than identifying only similarities, he uses contradictory or complementary Buddhist ideas to refine his understanding of Christian doctrine, as he explains in an interview:

Buddhism has helped me to rediscover, to deepen what it means when, in the New Testament—maybe it's the only definition of God that we find in the New Testament—when it says that "God is love." I think what Buddhism means by "interbeing" helps me appropriate what in our Christian terminology we mean when we say divine reality is love, and then that sets the stage for me—and I think for many Christians—for reappropriating one of our central symbols for God, spirit. So for me now when I say the word God, what I image, what I feel, thanks to Buddhism, is the interconnecting spirit—this ever-present spirit, this ever-present, interconnecting energy that is not a person, but is very personal, that this is the mystery that surrounds me, that contains me, and which I am in contact with in the Eucharist, in liturgies, and especially in meditation.[23]

In his best-selling book *Without Buddha I Could Not Be a Christian*, Knitter uses Buddhism as a flashlight to illuminate traditional Christian doctrines. He correlates the Buddhist doctrine of interbeing with the activity of the Holy Spirit, equates Christian salvation with Buddhist awakening, and puts Buddhist wisdom into conversation with Christian love. Relationships with non-Christians, he says, caused his shift from Christian to Buddhist-Christian identity: "We have an identity, but that identity in its origins and in its ongoing life comes to be and continues to flourish only through mixing it up with others. Hybrids are stronger, live longer, and have more fun than purebreds."[24]

Still, emphasizing how thought can influence choice doesn't make these complex religious bonds purely intellectual. People are attracted to multiple religions through their intellects, but the experience of spiritual practice often convinces them to stay. Complex religious bonds represent a holistic decision that includes the intellect but reaches beyond it. Spiritually fluid people in Java, Indonesia, for example, approach religion as a way of life rather than a system of belief. Legally, they must identify as monoreligious, choosing one of six officially recognized traditions (Christian Catholicism, Christian Protestantism, Buddhism, Islam, Hinduism, and Confucianism). But spiritually fluid Javanese choose one tradition for their government ID and maintain bonds to several traditions in daily life—even though monoreligious identities are legislated by law. Because many of these Javanese are children of interreligious marriages, their multiplicity is both chosen and inherited. All tend to reject institutional religious authority. They cultivate curiosity about other traditions, voicing a personal and immanent understanding of God. They don't present their complex religious bonds as the outcome of a cognitive process.[25]

Why, then, do cognitive explanations of multiplicity dominate? I see at least two reasons, both related to power. First, imagining choice as an intellectual process fits the dominant cultural ethos of Europe and the United States—both places where ideas are expected to be clear, coherent, and without contradiction. Scholars and religious leaders almost demand that spiritually fluid people justify themselves, logically and doctrinally, against criteria established by the traditions of European philosophy, Christian theology, and the academic industry that produces "legitimate" knowledge.

Second, most missionaries and academics who have written about multiple religious bonds address audiences that privilege logical, propositional thought. Institutional and cultural norms, as well as the technical languages and expectations of academic disciplines, lead them to offer rational accounts of their experiences. These accounts are rooted in, shaped by, and accountable to formal religious traditions and institutions—typically Christian—that value and reward ideas they assume can logically establish what's true or false (including doctrine). Even scholars who follow experiential, social, or collaborative pathways to complex religious bonds are likely to articulate multiplicity in the true/false discourse of academia and religious institutions. Thus, writing for the church and the academic world necessarily constrains—and perhaps sometimes enriches—how people describe and advocate for religious multiplicity.

These writers and thinkers are also influenced by shifting ideas about the self, recognizing that what we perceive as "individuals" have multiple facets. Each human being's identity contains myriad threads from the past, present, and future, braided into a whole that echoes the complexity and multiplicity of Mystery itself.[26] Past identities cannot be erased or lost entirely; they continue to influence who we are becoming now.

BRAIDED IDENTITIES

It's a given, then, that people who add new spiritual symbols, practices, and ideas to their lives—or convert formally to a new religion—cannot erase their earlier spiritual identities. New spiritual insights and commitments are accommodated, and sometimes integrated, into prior religious and spiritual understanding.[27] "My experience as a Jew entering the world of Buddhist meditation," writes Rabbi Sheila Weinberg, "is that my own spirit is so saturated with Jewish language and symbols that whatever insights and awareness I achieve are immediately translated into Jewish terms. The effect on me is an elucidation of Jewish texts and practices from the experience of the *dharma*. . . . My experience tells me that I can learn from other traditions and return to my Jewish center."[28]

Not all spiritually fluid people have a primary and a secondary tradition. For some, the traditions they claim share equal billing, equally important to their lives. The worldview of most spiritually fluid people provides a unified perspective informed by multiple traditions. Sallie King, a Buddhist-Christian scholar, describes it this way: "I do not respond to events 'as a Christian' or 'as a Buddhist,' but simply as a person conditioned by both."[29] The best-selling author Iyanla Vanzant, a Unity Church minister, is both a leader among black evangelical Christian women and an initiate to the Yoruba religion. She sees Jesus as an ancestor in the Yoruba sense.[30]

This dynamic—claiming equal allegiance to multiple traditions, as well as other manifestations of spiritual fluidity—partly reflects shifting notions of human identity in the West. Beginning with the European Renaissance, philosophers and, later, psychologists framed identity as static and individual. These assumptions helped shape ideas about religious singularity, a norm that demands commitment to a single tradition. But many scholars today see identity as dynamic, evolving, and interpersonal. It shifts over time and from one context to another, offering a more flexible understanding of what it means to be a person. Some argue that multiple identities are inevitable in today's world.[31]

If identity really is dynamic, then we should expect people's spiritualities to shift—and they are. In the Netherlands, for example, 24 percent of the population combines more than one religious tradition to create a "flexible religiosity" that honors commitments to multiple communities.[32] Around the world, religious bonds morph and adjust just as identities do, and people are shaped simultaneously by symbols and practices from multiple religious traditions as religious symbols speak not only across traditions but also to individuals. Sometimes, what people hear relates only tangentially to the traditions from which the symbols emerge.

Our spirits have both genealogy and geology: the resources of our past traditions provide structure, support, and, often, sustenance for our spirituality throughout life. Prior religious and spiritual identities stand beneath or behind current identities the way younger layers of rock rest atop older ones to form the ground below us. Early religious experiences and commitments show up in several ways: thoughts and beliefs, emotions and behaviors, and ethics and spiritual practices. Marie Romo, for example, embraces Hindu thought and some of its spiritual practices, but still uses monotheistic and Christian language to speak about Mystery:

God is my dad—my father—my husband, my friend. . . .
God is with me. . . . It's beautiful. . . . You know that he's
there, but we question him, we doubt him, we blame him,
or we just use him because [religion is] a pattern or form
that we're brought up with. . . . But he deserves your 100
percent attention. He deserves for you to try your best.
He deserves to know that he's your light, not anything
else. It's—excuse my French, but half-assed isn't good
enough. It has to be everything.

In terms of doctrine and practice, Marie emphasizes the overlap between Christianity and Hinduism. "God is unity," she says,
"not separation." Spiritually fluid people frequently address religious differences by seeking to create a positive and pragmatic
harmony or synthesis among these differences. Some spiritually
fluid people claim a primary religious tradition and supplement
it with the ideas and practices of a second, using the subordi-
nate tradition "to deepen their understanding of the first and
vice versa," writes Christian pastor and scholar Karen Georgia
Thompson. "Multiple religious belonging does not embrace a
second religion for study, but for practice and adherence."[33]

NAVIGATING THE TERRITORY OF CHOICE
People who choose multiplicity usually make the transition from
a season of curiosity to a season of engagement. Their initial exploration through reading and practice creates engagement that
leads to multiple participation or to identification with multiple
traditions. Suffering can increase during this period of multiple
practice and identity, but the benefits of being spiritually fluid
become clearer as well. During engagement, people encounter
Mystery in new and meaningful ways. But they can also suffer when choosing whether to hide or disclose their religious
multiplicity.

Much scholarly literature assumes that confusion accompanies the choice of multiple religious bonds. Catherine Cornille, for example, writes that "the experience of profound identification with one religion without losing one's attachment and commitment to another seems to be more often than not deeply confusing and spiritually unsettling."[34]

Confusion exists for some, but it seems less unsettling and more fleeting than scholars assume. I don't want to minimize confusion or the suffering that can accompany spiritual fluidity, but few religiously multiple people speak to me about being confused. They are more apt to emphasize the politics of truth claims; the tension of hiding and disclosing; a desire to help others understand how multiplicity works in their lives; and how being and becoming are more important than belief, behavior, and belonging.

THE POLITICS OF TRUTH CLAIMS

When spiritually fluid people feel confused, it's often related to claims of truth—especially for those whose original traditions make exclusive claims, like Christianity, Judaism, and Islam. Yet these people say that comparing doctrines and developing more sophisticated understanding are two of the greatest benefits of maintaining bonds with multiple traditions—even when doing so is painful. How, then, do they balance the pain with a sense of abundance that emerges from doctrinal differences? Expanding what counts as truth works for many.

Years ago, at a Pueblo dance in New Mexico, I began crying when drums called the dancers forth from the ceremonial kiva. My eyes welled up as soon as the first drum sounded, and silent tears ran down my cheeks as the dancers paraded past. Concerned, a Pueblo woman standing next to me asked, "Are you OK?"

"Yes," I said, wiping my cheeks with the fingers of both hands. "I don't know why I'm crying."

"I do," she answered.

I looked into her eyes. "Are you going to tell me?" I ventured.

"No," she said, and walked away.

Maybe she was grandstanding, claiming a spiritual wisdom that she didn't really have. Maybe she was teasing or playing a white tourist. And maybe she did know something I (still) don't know. Whatever her motivation, there was something true about my tears, and I experienced something true in that brief conversation. Even writing about the experience awakens a sense of wonder: my body responds to the memory with a broadening of my solar plexus and a drop of habitual tension from my shoulders. I cannot articulate a logical truth or insight about the moment, but it is real, good, and true nonetheless. To understand this experience, to make sense of what happened spiritually and religiously, we need to locate truth somewhere other than in doctrine and statements.

In this task, it can be useful to turn to Taoist Christian religion scholar John Berthrong, who argues that our understanding of religious truth "is curiously truncated in light of the breadth of human religious experience."[35] By focusing on doctrine and logic, he argues, we ignore aesthetic truth and embodied truth and the ways belief, beauty, and embodiment can overlap to enrich and inform each other.

Assertive or theoretical language about religious truth can be assessed logically as true or false in light of empirical evidence. These approaches make an assertion that people can argue about. (For example, the statement "There is no God but Allah," the central affirmation of Islam, serves as an assertive truth.) Exhibitive or aesthetic truth, on the other hand, occurs through beauty or performance; it is recognized rather than known cognitively and cannot be proven true or false. (For example, some people experience the ultimate in music or through the beauty of a sunset.) Aesthetic or exhibitive truth doesn't carry ideas, make assertions, or propose a particular viewpoint;

it is not logical or self-evident but conveys the real, the good, the true, and the beautiful beyond intellectual categories.

Active truth, on the other hand, relies on behavior—actions we understand, recognize, or respond to before assigning them intellectual meaning. The action "performs" a certain type of truth; the truth is made real through action, even though the action doesn't propose doctrines or make cognitive assertions about reality. (For example, rituals such as Christian baptism or a wedding ceremony are actions that create truth.)

Berthrong says no human language—logical, hypothetical, doctrinal, or statements about beauty and action—can capture religious or spiritual truth. All truth claims, he writes, "are only hypothetical because they can never be perfected, either empirically or metaphysically. What we have are not clear, distinct foundational theories of truth but rather corrigible hypotheses to be tested in the world as to their value and validity."[36] We know truth when we see it. "We are grasped by religious truth," he writes, "and act accordingly."[37]

Some spiritually fluid people say that multiplicity enhances, rather than challenges, their doctrinal grounding in a primary tradition. And conflicting claims about truth don't necessarily keep a person from practicing a coherent, unified spiritual path that does justice to both traditions.

Rose Drew, for example, studied six Buddhist-Christian practitioners, deeply exploring their experiences and beliefs. She concludes that "it is possible to follow a single spiritual path which is both authentically Buddhist and authentically Christian," especially if a person sees each tradition as a different but equally effective gateway to a single transcendent reality.[38] The places where the traditions intersect—where they agree on the nature of truth and reality—allow dual belongers to create and maintain a coherent worldview, Drew says, and allow both traditions to inform the individuals' spirituality without contradiction. She notes that spiritual leaders such as the Dalai Lama "accept that a person can be fully and beneficially committed to the practice of both traditions for as long as both are found to be helpful."[39] Focusing on spiritual truth known through action and beauty allows spiritually fluid people to celebrate complex religious bonds without the pressure of justifying themselves from intellectual or doctrinal perspectives. Berthrong's three ways of experiencing and recognizing truth can also help monoreligious people see more clearly how and why multiple traditions can speak to a person simultaneously.[40] Still, spiritually fluid people must decide for themselves when to disclose their complex religious bonds.

HIDING AND DISCLOSING

Disclosing multiplicity carries enormous risk. Spiritually fluid people often feel anxious when deciding whether to hide or disclose their religious multiplicity. Hiding it can protect them from judgment, conflict with others, and the need to justify themselves. But concealing multiplicity also compromises their honesty and authenticity; they're unable to be vulnerable with people they care about, especially family and religious leaders. "It's hard," Marie says. "I've taken myself [away] from a lot of things, which was very hard, and a lot of it was my family, because they're so close-minded. So when I'm with them, we talk, but we don't talk about religion." She frequently endures micro-aggressions from those who know about her complex religious bonds; if she talks about her spirituality, she's apt to be called "demonic." Her mother says her spiritual practice is "of the devil." Marie's response? "So be it. I am not afraid," she says. "I cut the ties of the [community's] tradition, I cut the ties of making people happy, because I knew God is my journey. It was him that got me through all the stuff."

Even people whose cultural capital and social privilege make it acceptable to disclose multiplicity—university faculty and other scholars, for example—are not immune to risk. The Vatican and

US bishops investigated Catholic theologian Peter Phan, for example, after he published *Being Religious Interreligiously*.[41] Although he wasn't formally disciplined, Catholic leaders warned that his ideas "could easily confuse or mislead the faithful."[42] Publicly disclosing exceptional spirituality—pushing against what's considered normal—can bring harsh consequences.

But disclosing multiplicity can also increase freedom and authenticity. The tension between potential risks and potential benefits makes it difficult to choose what, when, and how to disclose in personal relationships and in religious communities. Some people find themselves isolated after disclosure, shunned by those who do not accept complex religious bonds as life-giving. A monoreligious community can have a strong negative response to multiple religious bonds because "the religious community feels vulnerable if it cannot claim the believer fully," writes Lutheran Christian pastor and scholar Simone Sinn. "But also the believer is vulnerable as the community no longer regards him or her as a full member of the community, and thus she or he is pushed to the margins."[43]

These tensions are usually minor during the season of curiosity, when spiritually fluid people can downplay their interest in multiple religions as a lark, an experiment, an educational experience. (Sometimes they describe it this way even to themselves.) It's easiest to cope by passing as monoreligious. But during the season of engagement, when complex religious bonds become, shall we say, more complex, questions about disclosing and hiding multiplicity come to the fore. Spiritually fluid people no longer find it acceptable to pass as monoreligious, instead using code-switching or double consciousness (that is, knowing both who they are and how the dominant culture sees them; see chapter 5) to cope. As the risks of disclosure become clearer, it can feel more important to hide multiplicity.

The stress of disclosure generally becomes easier as people move into other seasons of multiplicity. As their spirituality evolves, hiding seems less important. By the time they enter the season of generativity, spiritually fluid people are no longer invested in keeping multiplicity a secret. Ruben, for example, primarily adopts double consciousness; he doesn't try to pass as monoreligious, but neither does he volunteer to disclose multiplicity unless the situation demands it. Nonetheless, the challenges of disclosure never totally disappear—especially in terms of finding the right words to describe spiritual fluidity.

BEING AND BECOMING VERSUS
BELIEF, BELONGING, AND BEHAVIOR

What people believe, their sense of belonging, and their religious behavior help us make sense of people's religious lives. These attributes are often visible in public, and they can be can be measured, verified, and assessed. Consequently, they are the primary categories researchers use to study lived religion. Belief relates to doctrinal commitments and assumptions about reality; belonging, to membership and participation in a religious community; and behavior, to worship attendance, spiritual disciplines, and other actions motivated by spiritual and religious commitment.

Focusing on belief, belonging, and behavior, however, limits our understanding of complex religious bonds. First, spiritual fluidity often shows up outside formal religious institutions and communities. Second, many spiritually fluid people pay little attention to beliefs or doctrines. Finally, traditional religious behaviors—worship attendance, ritual participation, spiritual disciplines—aren't the only ways people practice multiplicity. The tension between private piety—what we do at home, with friends, and in nature—and public religion comes into play, as do the differences between elite, institutional understanding and how people "do" religion in ordinary practice.

Religious nones don't pay much attention to religious belief, belonging, and behavior. They value being and becoming; for them, a person's spirituality relates to meaning, growth, transformation, and positive action. Relationships and personal integration matter more to them than do logical coherence, fidelity to a historical tradition, or orthodox understanding of religion and spirituality.

Spiritually fluid people also emphasize being and becoming. They privilege meaning, integration, and authentic relationship (to themselves, to others, to the world, and to Mystery). From the perspective of monoreligious spirituality, it's easy to label these values flaky, noncommittal, or New Age-y—in fact, spiritually fluid people are accustomed to that sort of micro-aggression. People with hybrid or multiple identities of many types, writes Canadian religion scholar Julius-Kei Kato, are often "viewed by monoculturals as half-way, half-done, unfinished, and lesser creatures." But, he continues, "a 'hybrid kind of religiosity' . . . is not half-way, half-done, or unfinished as monoculturals are wont to think. Instead, hybrid entities have an integrity all their own."[44]

You can't accurately measure spiritually fluid people, then, with a monoreligious yardstick. Our accounts of contemporary spirituality and religion must account for the value people place on spiritual being and spiritual becoming as much as on doctrine and tradition.

CHOOSING TO FLOURISH

In the end, people choose complex religious bonds because multiplicity offers them more benefits than drawbacks. The difficulties and occasional suffering do not outweigh the gifts that come from straddling traditions. Spiritual fluidity can enhance clarity, increase personal and communal freedom, and allow for mutual transformation among religious traditions. The integrity of complex religious bonds doesn't disappear just because some people see them as contradictory, syncretic, or impossible. Choosing religious multiplicity, in fact, can be a means of resisting demands that we be singular, logically coherent, and faithful to tradition as defined by others.

CHAPTER THREE

Receiving

THINK FOR A MINUTE about going to bed when you were a child. You probably had some sort of bedtime ritual. Maybe your parents sang you to sleep. Maybe you kissed each member of your family or knelt in prayer or brushed your teeth before going to bed. My mother would tuck me in, put my book on the nightstand, turn off the bedroom light, and leave the door open a crack so light from the hallway could spill into my room. Informal bedtime rituals like these happen around the world as parents try to quiet children's minds and bodies for the transition from day to night. In some families, these rituals include shared evening prayer. Sita Dookeran and her siblings, for example, recited the Lord's Prayer with her parents at bedtime, followed by the family's Hindu benediction: "Goodnight, sweet dreams, Sita-ram!" Enveloped by Christian prayer and a Hindu blessing, the five children crossed the threshold of sleep on the words of Jesus and the names of Sita and Rama—the Hindu goddess of virtue, abundance, and well-being, and her husband, the god of compassion and devotion.

Until Sita (the girl, not the goddess) started school, she thought every home honored Jesus and Hindu gods at the same time.

"As I got older, I became more aware," she remembers, "kind of realizing: Oh, OK, the Christian part is the part that fits in with society, the part I can mention in school. The Hindu stuff is the stuff I keep to myself. . . . I remember in school, if people asked, 'What did you do on the weekend?,' I felt comfortable saying we went to church. I wouldn't have felt comfortable saying we went to puja, which is one of the words for prayer gatherings in the Hindu faith. So I just sort of instinctively learned to hide it, because it wasn't—because if I had said it, they wouldn't have known what I was talking about."

Like many who inherit complex religious bonds from family or culture, Sita, the daughter of Caribbean immigrants to Canada, cannot separate being spiritually fluid from her experiences of race, culture, and identity in the mostly white world of Winnipeg in the 1970s. Race was a volatile issue in Canadian politics at the time, and as a person of South Asian heritage, Sita looked different from her classmates. Her parents, as Caribbean immigrants, not only looked different from the majority population, but also spoke with an accent, cooked unfamiliar foods, and dressed in ways that set them apart.

"I remember sitting around in a circle in about, maybe, grade three, and for some reason, the teacher was having everybody say what they had for dinner the night before," Sita says. "People were going around and saying things like hamburgers, hotdogs, maybe pasta, or something like that. And I knew that we had curry chicken, because . . . we ate that at least once a week. And I got more nervous . . . and when it came to my turn, I just said hamburger. I didn't want to be different."

Fitting in was easier among Hindus, who mostly accepted Jesus as a spiritual teacher. But Christians made it clear that Hindu and Indo-Caribbean cultures were not acceptable at church, even as church attendance increased the family's sense of community acceptance. This created inner conflicts and personal suffering for Sita, especially as an adolescent and a young adult. She didn't want to be different, but neither did she want to hide or erase her family's Hinduism.

"It would have felt like a deep betrayal," she says, "because it was who our family was. My connection, my deep connection,

to my mother was part of all the rituals we did together and part
of everything that she was teaching to me. And that involved
cooking, right? It was the rituals and the way we dressed and
the prayers we said, all of that, but making food is a big part of
the prayer ritual. We would make certain holy foods . . . and put
it on the altar during prayers so that the food would be blessed,
and then we would mix that little bit of food in with the bigger
batch, and after the prayer, we'd give it to everybody who attended. So food and religion are very much connected."

WHO INHERITS MULTIPLICITY?

Some people choose multiplicity as a spiritual path, but most—
like Sita—are born into it. Complex religious bonds are a heritage from family, from culture, and often from a historical legacy
of migration, conquest, and colonization by people whose religion was different from local traditions. In Brazil, for instance,
Afro-Brazilians and Brazil's indigenous people struggled to
maintain their original beliefs after receiving new names—often
the names of their Christian slave owners—during involuntary
baptism. (Their experience reminds us that sometimes the sacrament of baptism functions more as a ritual of empire than as
a warm and fuzzy moment of receiving new life and becoming
part of the church and Christian faith.) Maintaining multiple
bonds—practicing indigenous traditions while participating in
Christian worship—allowed some indigenous people to preserve their identities and resist colonial violence.

People who inherit multiplicity cannot disown multiplicity.
They include Japanese who engage in Shinto, Buddhist, and
Christian rituals at different moments in life; the Bai people of
China, whose altars include Buddhist, Taoist, and local Ben-
zhuist deities; Bolivian shamans who worship Catholic saints
alongside local gods; or Western interfaith children raised in
both Judaism and Christianity.[1] Most who inherit multiplicity
don't want to disown their traditions; for example, 26 percent

of Nepalis in Great Britain, when given a choice, identify with multiple religions.[2] Even if people who inherit complex religious bonds don't like or appreciate them, religious multiplicity is deeply embedded in their families and cultures. The people around them accept and expect spiritual fluidity.

Many people who inherit complex religious bonds live simultaneously in both traditions, unwilling or unable to distinguish one religious part of themselves from the other. "Without Islam," writes Amaryllis Puspabening, whose mother is Muslim and father is Catholic, "I may never have known God, and without Catholicism, I may have never grown to love Him. One can never know nor love God completely—and so I shall continue to learn."[3] Others who inherit multiplicity talk about changing "spiritual garments" according to circumstances, the way some of us wear a suit or skirt to work and flip-flops to the beach.[4] People born into multiplicity might adopt a single religion later in life, becoming monoreligious, but they are still influenced by the traditions that shaped their childhood. Often, children born into a legacy of spiritual fluidity assume (as Sita did) that everyone mixes religious and spiritual traditions or adopts different spiritual customs at different times.

For those who inherit complex religious bonds, multiplicity doesn't feel inherently transgressive. It doesn't seem exotic, and it doesn't initially create cognitive dissonance or anxiety about conflicting truths. Inherited multiplicity doesn't begin with curiosity about a "foreign" religion. It never feels unfamiliar or like crossing a boundary, and accepting it doesn't require mental gymnastics. For those born into multiplicity, being spiritually fluid is less a cognitive or intellectual challenge than an embodied and performed reality. Spiritual fluidity is their *life*, and most who inherit it don't need to reconcile the traditions or identify the places where the traditions intersect; they themselves *are* the intersections others seek. They are crossroads that prove the possibility, goodness, and value of complex religious bonds—the place where personal stories, cultural realities, and religious canons intersect.

This chapter focuses on people we could call *spiritual hybrids*, those born into, or inheriting, religious multiplicities. (Many spiritually fluid people also inherit other multiplicities, including multiple races, cultures, ethnicities, nationalities, and social roles.) For people who inherit multiplicity, navigating complexity and ambiguity is second nature. Curiosity rarely comes into play; they're born into, and grow up in, engagement with complex religious bonds.

Unlike people who choose multiplicity, spiritual hybrids don't cross borders or travel between traditions; the traditions dance, overlap, and merge in their families and communities. The different religious homes of those who inherit complex religious bonds function like neighborhoods in a single city. The people see themselves not as immigrants or refugees moving from one tradition to another but as natural-born citizens of each religion. Both territories belong to them; each territory is home, the way some people live in Brooklyn and work in Manhattan: two places, one city, no restrictions on travel. People who inherit complex religious bonds don't need to slip across boundaries in secret, the way those who choose multiplicity sometimes do. Those who inherit or receive complex religious bonds travel between traditions in broad daylight, and they can be surprised when others want or need a passport or visa to enter a new religious territory. Multiple belonging is a birthright, a cultural resource; they don't question it. It's the norm.[5]

PUBLIC CATHOLICS,
PRIVATE *SANTEROS* AND *SANTERAS*

Consider Christian theologian Miguel De La Torre. He grew up with Catholic parents who also practiced Santeria, an Afro-Caribbean religion. Both his parents served as Santeria priests to the Cuban refugee community in Queens, where Miguel grew up.

As an *hijo de Eleggua* (child of Eleggua, one of the orishas, or gods), he was expected to become a Santeria priest like his parents. "My family and I followed the precepts of the orishas; paradoxically, I also went to a Catholic elementary school in Queens, New York," he writes. "I took my first communion, participated in weekly confession, and was confirmed at Blessed Sacrament Church, even though at night, crowds would visit our apartment to consult the gods."[6]

For Miguel, living "in between" Santeria and the church was simply the way things were. In fact, it was central to his community's survival in a new country:

> There was never any confusion in my mind, in my parents' mind, or in the minds of those visiting our house-temple regarding the difference between what was done at the Irish church down the street and what was done in our apartment. From an early age, my parents explained to me that the rituals we participated in could not be revealed to the priests or the nuns because they were "confused" about how God works, and if they found out that we had *el conocimiento* (the knowledge), I would be expelled from the school. Yet when I asked what we were, they would reply without hesitating, as if by rote: "We are apostolic Roman Catholics, but we believe in our own way." . . .
>
> While there was no confusion among those of us practicing Santeria concerning the difference between us and the priests and nuns, still an ambiguous religiosity developed, fusing the elements of these diverse traditions in order to resist what was perceived to be the danger of assimilating into the dominant Euroamerican ethos.[7]

Miguel De La Torre no longer practices Santeria, but his religious self was shaped tremendously by the *santeros* and *santeras* responsible for his spiritual growth as a child and young adult.

"If we are all influenced by our social contexts," he writes, "then these individuals have left a permanent mark on my spiritual being, even though I no longer participate in this religious tradition."[8]

Throughout his life, Miguel has been influenced by the religious multiplicity he inherited from his parents, his community, and the elders who attended to his spiritual development. He is not alone. For many, identifying as spiritually fluid or religiously multiple hinges on social processes: a person receives a spiritual identity-of-the-moment from what's happening at a particular time, taking cues from the people, the physical environment, and the expectations that surround them. Their religious identities shift as the individuals engage in different relationships or enter new spaces (literal and metaphorical). It's as if spirituality is a human product: a cultural artifact or tool fashioned for particular purposes.

For this reason, I think of inheritance as a primarily social or relational pathway into a spiritually fluid life. The relationships that sustain inherited multiplicities—relationships among ancestors, institutions, languages, and cultures—exist prior to the spiritually fluid person. They not only transmit complex religious bonds, but also create an ecology that sustains spiritually fluid people and contributes to their flourishing.

People receive or inherit complex religious identities in a variety of ways. Some people are born to parents from two religious traditions. Others grow up in locales where culture and practice make spiritual fluidity a norm. A few hold their spiritual identities lightly enough to shift from one tradition to another in response to cues from the people around them. There's an element of choice in these processes, of course; the categories of religious choice, heritage, and invitation are not pure or exclusive. But the pathway of inheritance is different from the pathways of choice and invitation. Inheritance includes a communal expectation and approval of fluid or flexible religious identities, and this communal attitude precedes individual choice. This supportive ethos doesn't necessarily exist in the pathways of choice and invitation. Therefore, people who receive complex religious identities understand multiplicity primarily as a heritage and a resource rather than a response to Mystery or a decision based on ethics, intellect, or personal preference.

GROWING UP IN AN INTERFAITH FAMILY

Many people who inherit complex religious bonds grow up in an interfaith family. They have a Jewish mother and a Christian father, for example, and grow up attending church and synagogue. Others might have a Christian mother and a Hindu father and refer to their family religion as Chinduism. Still others are raised by parents of two religious traditions, with aunts, uncles, grandparents, and cousins from several other traditions. In North America, the term *interfaith marriage* once referred almost exclusively to Jewish-Christian unions, but now, interfaith families around the world are increasingly complex—as are the challenges they face. How do you plan a wedding when the groom and his mother are Hindu, his father is Catholic, and the bride and her family are Muslim?[9] How do you parent Hindu-Muslim children in India, or Buddhist-Muslim children in Myanmar, places where violence sometimes pits those religious communities against each other? How do a Christian mother and a Muslim father negotiate the religious education and coming-of-age rituals of their children?

Interfaith marriages increasingly result in people who identify as interfaith or spiritually fluid. The experience has become so common, in fact, that television's *Today* show recently aired a segment about interfaith families. In the mid-1960s, about 20 percent of US marriages were interfaith; now the number is approaching 50 percent. In interfaith marriages that include children, fewer than half raise their daughters and sons in a single religious tradition.[10] People like Sita Dookeran, who grew up with two religious traditions central to family life, show up more often in public life. Former US president Barack Obama, for example, grew up with a Christian mother and a Muslim father who was also shaped by Hinduism and traditional religions. Chelsea Clinton, a United Methodist Christian, married Marc Mezvinsky, a Jew; their two children are poster children for people born into complex religious bonds. Nobel Prize winner Bob Dylan grew up Jewish, raised his children in the Jewish tradition, and continued to attend synagogue with them after he himself converted to Christianity. When *Rolling Stone* asked Dylan whether his faith had changed over the years, the seventy-one-year-old singer said, "Certainly it has, o ye of little faith. Who's to say that I even have any faith or what kind? I see God's hand in everything. Every person, place and thing, every situation. I mean, we can have faith in just about anything."[11]

People who inherit religious multiplicity often refuse to choose between the family's various religious traditions, because each tradition plays a significant role in identity, family, and racial-ethnic heritage. Yet being born into an interfaith family presents challenges. Some research suggests that interfaith marriages are less satisfying to spouses and more likely to result in divorce than are marriages in which both partners share a religion. Journalist and commentator Naomi Schaefer Riley argues that this interfaith challenge exists because these couples enter marriage without sufficient attention to spiritual, doctrinal, and practical issues—the precise issues that can divide them as their children grow older.[12]

Some interfaith marriages, on the other hand, embrace differences rather struggling with them. Author Susan Katz Miller, for example, grew up in a Jewish-Christian household, and she rejects the idea that children and parents must make an either-or choice between traditions. A second-generation interfaith person raising a third generation of interfaith children, Miller celebrates the benefits of "being both": promoting transparency about differences, encouraging family unity, giving equal weight to extended family, sidestepping Jewish concerns about whether the religion is inherited from the mother or the father, providing literacy in both religions, and promoting cultural harmony.

Miller says that interfaith families need communities, clergy, rituals, and education that affirm their experiences, and a growing number of such communities and clergy exist (as she documents in her book *Being Both: Embracing Two Religions in One Interfaith Family*). There's the Interfaith Families Project in Washington, DC; the national Dovetail Institute for Interfaith Family Resources; the Interfaith Community chapters in Boston, New York City, New Jersey, and other locations; the Jewish Catholic Couples Dialogue Group in Chicago; the Interfaith Family School in Chicago; and informal interfaith family education cooperatives in the Bay Area. Yet Miller also insists that the broader culture needs to affirm the experiences of interfaith families; they can't just support each other. To that end, she proposes a Bill of Rights for Interfaith People, which is based on the Bill of Rights for People of Mixed Heritage, a document developed by the multirace psychologist Maria Root:

I have the right:

- not to justify my existence
- not to keep the religions separate within me
- not to justify my religious legitimacy
- not to be responsible for people's discomfort with my religious ambiguity
- to identify myself differently than strangers expect
- to identify myself differently than how my parents identify me
- to identify myself differently than my brothers and sisters

- to identify myself differently in different situations
- to create a vocabulary to communicate about being interfaith
- to change my religious identity over my lifetime— and more than once
- to have loyalties to and identify with more than one group of people
- to freely choose whom I befriend and love[13]

These rights seem appropriate for any spiritually fluid people, and Miller argues that children born to interfaith families are uniquely positioned to reduce religious intolerance and promote religious peace. "We have given both of our children love for two cultures and literacy in two religions," Miller writes. "We have given them the gifts of seeing connections and contrasts, of going beyond embrace of the other to actually embody the other. We have given them the gift of joyful interfaithness."[14]

Another benefit of being spiritually fluid is always having a second religious authority and second source of comfort when one tradition becomes confusing, illogical, or frightening. Sita Dookeran invokes the metaphor of family to make sense of spiritual fluidity: "I'm getting this image in my head of a single-parent family as opposed to a two-parent family. Kids are often really, really close with that single parent because it's all they have. They can't see fault; it would destroy their world. But if they have two parents, they can say, 'Well, my mom is a bit of a nut sometimes. . . . That's okay: My dad is cool,' or whatever."

Religious scholar Abraham Vélez de Cea, a Buddhist-Christian, likewise uses the metaphor of family to describe complex religious bonds. He emphasizes that he's fully capable of loving both traditions at the same time just as people love both their parents or all their children simultaneously. "I prefer to view the religions to which I belong as parents who give me life, guidance and protection, or as children to whom I serve with patience, unconditional love and undivided commitment," he writes.[15]

GROWING UP IN A SPIRITUALLY FLUID CULTURE

In some parts of the world—Pacific Rim countries come to mind, along with India and some parts of Africa—complex religious bonds are less a family issue than a cultural reality. In Java, for example, Muslims at the national mosque (designed by a Christian architect) call people to prayer with an indigenous drum decorated not only with Arabic prayers but also with Sanskrit and Hindu terms and symbols.[16] Like the Javanese, I suspect most people in the world live in environments where being spiritually fluid is an everyday experience; it's so expected and unremarkable that they don't even recognize what they experience as religious multiplicity. In these settings, religions overlap: Hindus and Muslims make offerings at a Christian church, Jesus is acknowledged as a prophet at the mosque, Taoist gods hunker down on altars alongside Buddha images, Pueblo dancers in indigenous ceremony are blessed by a Catholic priest. In India, a common shrine culture leads Christians, Hindus, and Muslims to pray to the same saints at the same sites without distinguishing which tradition "owns" a particular saint or shrine. In Chennai, Muslims and Hindus pray at the Catholic shrine of St. Antony; Hindu devotees of Jesus, called *Christ bhakta*, worship at the shrine; and most of the devotional materials that pilgrims leave, including Krishna cradles for fertility and material gifts to evoke St. Antony's power, are Hindu in origin.

People who receive spiritual fluidity from their cultures often take a functional approach to religion: different traditions are responsible for, or have influence over, different parts of life.[17] You might go to the Buddhist temple to have your fortune told or to get help for your anxiety, bow before a Taoist-Confucian altar to honor the ancestors and ask them for good luck, and hold your wedding at a Christian church. A Buddhist temple houses altars to Taoist gods and Confucian ancestors. A Christian woman makes an offering to a tree spirit outside her office during the full moon, and she burns incense to her ancestors on the family altar each day. In China, Vietnam, and other parts of the Asian continent, the three traditions of Buddhism, Taoism, and Confucianism are considered complementary.[18] Belief in one doesn't require the rejection of others. This coexistence of traditions doesn't mean there are no conflicts between them or that some people in these situations don't argue that people should only practice one tradition, but overall, religious multiplicity is a norm.

In South Korea, a practice known as *reverence of heaven*— influenced by indigenous spirituality, shamanism, Taoism, and Buddhism—is central to people's spiritual lives, including those who identify as Christian. "Korean people improvise their collective sense of divinity 'attuned to' the traditional Heaven reverence," writes Christian theologian (and Presbyterian pastor) Insook Lee:

> Although this traditional Heaven reverence has never become an organized system of doctrines, rituals, and rites, it has permeated Korean people's religiosity. Instead of functioning as a systematized religion, Heaven reverence has been a background spirituality, a kind of basso continuo on which Korean people improvise their sense of the transcendent and create various melodies that play above it. They pick snippets from multiple traditions: Shamanism, Taoism, Buddhism, Confucianism, and, more recently, Christianity. Rather than assimilating them into an absolute, systemized, and logically coherent system, Korean people bring those traditions together in such a way that the multiple but distinct melodies and rhythms are heard simultaneously.[19]

Even in nations where religious singularity is a cultural norm, like the United States, some locales—especially those influenced by immigration and colonialism—expect people to engage in religious multiplicity. One example is Hawaii, where religion is less a matter of belief or affiliation than of relationship with friends, families, and neighbors. When an eighty-year-old Chinese man died in Honolulu, for example, his funeral included Christian, Taoist, and indigenous Hawaiian elements. Each part was important to his spiritual identity, even though he didn't officially belong to any tradition or congregation. "It is part of the local culture to affiliate with multiple religions as a way of connecting with your neighbors, friends and acquaintances," says Charles Buck, the United Church of Christ pastor who hosted the funeral. He continues:

> If you are Christian and your Buddhist friend dies, you will go to the service and participate in the Buddhist rites because it is the only right, the loving, thing to do. For many in Hawai'i, multiple religious belonging is not so much adherence to multiple faiths, but affiliation with the people who identify with these faiths. Ultimately, it is about building relationship and community—important and necessary values in the diverse and complex local culture that is Hawai'i.[20]

These spiritually fluid locales and ceremonies challenge the idea that each religion is a distinct entity with clear boundaries. It's easy to attribute this idea, and the expectation of religious singularity, to the dominance of monotheistic traditions: Christianity, Judaism, and Islam. But the myth of religious singularity was created in part by Western scholars who championed a world-religions approach to scholarship, treating Buddhism, Christianity, Hinduism, Islam, Judaism, and other traditions as monolithic and mutually exclusive entities. This simplistic approach ignores how traditions overlap in people's lives, both now and throughout history.

Rather than assuming that different religions belong to different parts of the world, with fixed borders between traditions, I find it more useful—and more accurate—to think in terms of "strategic religious participation."[21] This view, promoted by religion scholar Paul Hedges, suggests that people draw from the features of a shared religious landscape, taking part in the practices of a variety of religious traditions to meet specific goals. In other words, people in such settings see different religious traditions as providing specialized resources for particular spiritual concerns; as a result, they draw on the resources that are useful in their situations.

Focusing on strategic religious participation rather than on belief or belonging allows us to see religions as organic and always shifting ways of life. People participate in multiple spiritualities, that is, "overlapping systems of culture, rather than voluntaristic, mutually-exclusive, and discrete" traditions.[22] If religion is an experience rather than a set of beliefs, all sorts of things become possible. Catholic priest Raimon Panikkar, who inherited multiplicity from parents having two religious traditions, puts it this way: "Christ was not half man and half God, but fully man and fully God. In the same way, I consider myself 100 percent Hindu and Indian, and 100 percent Catholic and Spanish. How is that possible? By living religion as an experience rather than as an ideology."[23]

People who grow up in spiritually fluid cultures or families have an intuitive way of adapting new religious ideas and practices to their existing spiritual lives. Tantric master Yogi Chen, for example, a Chinese practitioner of esoteric Buddhism, immigrated to the United States toward the end of his life. His encounters with Christianity as the dominant religion in his new home led him to create "A Ritual of Fire Sacrifice to the Five Saints of Christianity," in which he made offerings to the Vedic fire god, Agni; to Jesus, God, and Mary; and to male and female apostles of Jesus. The offerings included bread and wine, the elements of the Christian sacrament of the Eucharist (or the Lord's Supper). Yogi Chen adopted Catholicism's Stations of the Cross—a circuit of remembering the sufferings of Jesus —as a type of mandala, in which Jesus was an avatar, or manifestation, of the Buddhist bodhisattva Guanyin.[24] Some Hindu-Christian practitioners also understand Jesus as an avatar of God, and in Bangladesh a community known as Isa Imandars (the Faithful of Jesus) worships Jesus while retaining the language and other forms of Islam. This community accepts Mohammed as prophet and worships Christ as God. In fifteenth-century India, the poet Kabir adopted Islamic imagery to write from a perspective that was simultaneously Hindu and Muslim, although he did not "belong" to either tradition.[25]

Sometimes, people who inherit complex religious bonds "pass" as monoreligious: they function as Christians in Christian settings, for example, and as Hindus in Hindu settings. They usually don't intend to mislead others, but choose (sometimes subconsciously) to foreground certain facets of their religious selves while keeping others in the background. This tendency has three benefits: it honors and reflects community norms, it maintains and affirms relationships, and it allows spiritually fluid people to remain flexible about how to express their religious and spiritual commitments. People who choose to be spiritually fluid (rather than inheriting it) can also adopt this strategy, reflecting the religious identity of the people and communities around them at any moment. I see this practice of bringing certain types of spirituality to the foreground according to circumstances as another form of receiving religious identity—although people might choose multiplicity, they also receive their spiritual identity-of-the-moment from the expectations of the people around them. As a spiritually fluid pastor and chaplain, I know this process—and its complexities—well.

RECEIVING IDENTITY

It's ironic to write about "being" both Buddhist and Christian, because the traditions toss out the idea that we can claim an identity for ourselves.[26] Identity, for Christians, comes from God through *baptism*, a sacrament involving prayer and water. (For Reformed Christians like me, baptism isn't a human choice but is a visible sign that God has claimed and cleansed us: it's God's action, not ours.) Buddhists reject identity altogether; the doctrine of no-self (anatta) instead affirms that nothing—not people, not flowers, not animals, not houses, not nations— has an inherent self or identity. Instead, everything is imperma-nent, impersonal, and—if we try to hold on to it as something "real"—dissatisfying. For Buddhists, it's a delusion to believe the self exists, and we suffer if we insist that identity is stable or lasting.[27]

But this ephemeral state is not our experience; day by day, our identities don't seem temporary, empty, or erased. They en-dure from year to year and decade to decade, chiseled into us by the world; they carry our values and wisdom and preferences and relationships. Identities define how we understand our-selves and how we are understood by others. They allow us to navigate the world successfully, relating to others and to reality. They are a tool for navigating life. Sometimes, my identity seems so full it could overflow, the way water spills over a stopped-up sink. We can't do without identities; we need them.

If we need identities to be fully human and to live well with others, then how do we make sense of these religious truths? What would it mean to live as if identity doesn't really exist and/or comes from somewhere beyond us? It's helpful, from my perspective, to see identity as a collection of meanings, ne-gotiated with others. My identity doesn't come from inside me but emerges *between* me and others during shared experiences like washing dishes, following traffic laws, honoring parents, celebrating birthdays, attending funerals, and coordinating our energy and skills to achieve goals and get work done. Who I am emerges from relationships first; only later do I take into myself the meanings that form identity, where they become a resource or tool for navigating the world and meeting goals.

If this is true in any sense—if who I am emerges from what I do with the meanings I receive from others—then I am what I do in response to the world. That assertion makes identity something practiced or performed rather than something we are or believe. This way of understanding identity makes sense to me; spiritual practices, for example—the things we do to stay connected with Mystery or to reflect what is ultimately true—often reveal religious identity better than what we believe (or say we believe) or which religious institution(s) we "belong to."[28] The importance of religious and spiritual action, rather than belief and belonging, came to the forefront of the 2016 presidential campaign when Donald Trump publicly identified as Christian, but Pope Francis pointed to the candidate's words and actions as inherently *not* Christian. In light of how Trump performs his religious and spiritual identity in daily life, the pope called that identity into question.

So what does it look like to perform or practice religious identity when you have bonds to more than one spiritual tradition?

DANCING WITH DEATH

Two stories show how I received, performed, and practiced "my" religious identities as a Buddhist, Christian, and Buddhist/Christian in certain circumstances.[29] They are stories about dancing with death through my religious identities and by caring for others. The stories seem appropriate because they involve friendliness and dying, the only types of meditation that, according to a Tibetan Buddhist text, are consistently beneficial in every way.[30] Death and grief also have a way of showing how interconnected we are. These deaths taught me how my Buddhist, Christian, and Buddhist/Christian identities are flexible, emerging from relationships and human predicaments. My religious selves are caught up in lives beyond my own.

Saying Goodbye to a Husband and Father

Years ago as a chaplain, I was called to the bedside of the dying patriarch of an Asian American family. The family had come to the United States as refugees of a devastating war, and the family members born in the United States considered themselves American first and Asian second, while the parents and older children tried to maintain their homeland cultures. When I entered the room, I wore my Christian identity on my sleeve: I was a chaplain, after all! I had a Bible in my hand, a cross on a chain around my neck, and a firm conviction that I could escort the patient and his family into the territory of death.

But here's the catch: the family had no idea why I was there. They didn't know what a chaplain was, and bedside visits to the dying weren't a part of their Buddhist tradition. We didn't share a language, and no one responded to the cues I offered about my role. We smiled at each other in awkward silence, ignoring the failing body in the bed, until a much younger son arrived. He spoke to his mother and siblings in Vietnamese, and then he turned to me. "We are grateful you came to visit our father," he said, "but we do not need a Christian pastor here. My father is Buddhist."

Without speaking, I placed my hands palm-to-palm in front of my chest in a namaste gesture. Then I began chanting in Pali, the sacred language of Theravada Buddhism: *Namo tassa bhagavato arahato samma sambuddhasam* ("Homage to the holy one, the self-enlightened one, the one who is totally enlightened"). The feeling in the room changed instantly. Awkwardness melted away. Family members bowed in prayer. Each child approached the father and blessed him; then the wife blessed each of the children, offered a long prayer in Vietnamese, and invited me to pray in English. Their time of grief and confusion became an opportunity to make merit for their dying husband and father—an important practice in Buddhism. We became a sacred community: *Sangham jivitam yava nibbanam saranam gacchami*—to life's end, until I reach *nibbana*, my refuge is the sangha, the community of Buddhist practitioners.

In that hospital room, I seemed to have arrived as a Christian pastor, an identity created through denominational formation and daily encounters with patients and families who were fundamentalist and evangelical Christians. I departed as a Buddhist deacon, an identity informally internalized through my devotional and congregational lives—which themselves were the results of social processes that began centuries before my birth—and then evoked by, performed before, and embraced by a sympathetic audience. For the family, my unexpected identity carried great meaning and some comfort. For me, it required a nimble shift to reveal, responsibly and authentically, the Buddhist facets of my "self." It can happen the other way, too: bringing the Christian facets to the fore when the Buddhist dimensions aren't sufficient.

Singing Richard to Heaven

Years later, late one night, I visited a friend dying at a local hospital. The Sunday before, I had greeted him in the lobby of our church, and he had said that it would be useful to talk together about his diagnosis. Before we could meet, he entered the hospital. Now he was in a coma, and I felt sad and guilty as I rode the elevator to his floor. I knew we couldn't talk, but I wanted to sit beside him quietly and practice *metta bhavana*, a Buddhist meditation on loving-kindness. Sending that energy would ease my guilt and, I hoped, ease his passage from one world to another.

I went late at night because I didn't want to see anyone else. Richard was single, and his biological family lived far away. I reasoned that church members who loved him would be at home with their families and that in the stillness of the oncology unit,

Richard and I could share a sense of solitude. I might even stay until morning, I thought. But when I stepped into his room, I saw a half dozen people sitting quietly around his bed.

They looked at me expectantly. I knew I had intruded into a circle of chosen family, brothers who had surrounded and supported Richard for decades. Together they had traveled the world, celebrated holidays, and lived through the ups and downs of careers, broken hearts, health crises, and hot Texas summers. Now they surrounded him in the process of dying. I immediately decided I wouldn't stay long but would stand far from the bed, send one ripple of loving-kindness around the room, and step into the hallway. Focusing on my breath, I turned my eyes in turn to each man in the room, watching him watch his dying friend, while I silently prayed: *May you be at peace; may you be free of suffering; may you be well and happy.* No one seemed to notice me until I turned my gaze to the man beside me.

He was a mutual friend from church, someone who knew Richard especially well. He knew I was a pastor, and when I turned to him, he looked into my eyes over the rim of his glasses, leaned close, and took my arm. "Don't you dare leave," he whispered, "without having a word of prayer with us."

Without another word, we joined hands and stepped toward the bed. The others joined us. Forming a circle around Richard, we moved into Christian worship. We read scripture, sang hymns, laid hands on our friend. We anointed his head with moisturizer and released him to God. Each man spoke a tender farewell and blessing, witnessed by the others. Members of the choir arrived, singing an a cappella version of John Bell's hymn "The Last Journey": "From the falter of breath, through the silence of death . . ."[31] Richard died the next morning.

I hadn't identified myself overtly as Christian when I entered Richard's hospital room. In fact, I had intended to practice a key spiritual discipline in the Buddhist traditions. But his friends invited me to perform a different identity: "Promise you won't leave without having a word of prayer." That hidden identity came forth in the space between one man's lips, teeth, and tongue and another man's ear; it became real as it was performed and accepted by the gathered community. "O blest communion, fellowship divine! . . . All are one in Thee, for all are Thine. Alleluia, Alleluia!"[32]

IDENTITY, FAITH, AND SOCIAL PROCESSES
Each deathbed encounter invited me to highlight different facets of my religious and spiritual selves. I entered each room with one identity in mind, but the people I met needed something different. I received an alternate identity from the cues offered by others; at those moments, I functioned like a mirrored gem reflecting the primary religious identity of the gems nearest me. I practiced or performed my religious self in new ways to reflect the people nearby, just as mirror neurons in your brain reflect the emotions of the person across from you, giving rise to empathy.[33]

It was relationships, not belief or doctrine or belonging, that shaped my religious-identity-of-the-moment. The relationships allowed new possibilities to arise between me and the families whose loved ones were dying. When a son said, "My father is Buddhist," and a grieving friend whispered, "Promise you won't leave," the words created space for a religious identity that hadn't been front and center. None of us intended for this change to happen, but I received their words as invitations to practice my religious self differently. At those moments, my religious identity wasn't objective (something they knew or saw) or subjective (inside me or an identity I knew for certain). It was shared, located between and among people in a hospital room.

I internalized and performed those identities-as-possibilities for pragmatic reasons: to relate more effectively to the people around me and to relieve suffering. In each case, an identity that lay dormant beneath or behind our interactions woke up to become a tool for relating to each other in new ways. I created, shared, and coordinated my religious and spiritual identities through the words and actions of communities gathered to grieve and comfort a person who was dying.

For me, it's comforting to know that religious identities can be reoriented into patterns of meaning and relationship—patterns that are useful in the moment. Spiritual identities can be skilled and evolving performances of particular types of religious meaning. By allowing my spiritual identity to be fluid—shifting it to meet the needs of the moment—I demonstrated a certain flexibility, a knowing *how to be* a certain religious person rather than a knowing *that I am* a Buddhist or a Christian.[34]

If religious and spiritual identities are interactive, shifting in the moment and performed through relationships and in communities, then they are not only the mental, emotional, or spiritual properties of an individual but also social and relational processes. Our religious and spiritual experiences—the times when we sense the active presence of Mystery—are made real through relationships. They are created and made concrete in new ways when we share them with one another.

RELATIONSHIPS, RELIGION, AND MULTIPLE
REALITIES: BUDDHIST AND CHRISTIAN INSIGHT

Buddhists probably aren't bothered by the thought that religious identity is inherited or received, emerging from relationships rather than from a person's inner self. The idea resonates with the Buddhist doctrine of interbeing (*paticca samuppada*): This is, because that is; this is not, because that is not. Seeing the (nonexistent) self as relational, kaleidoscopic, and always shifting can be a fundamental Buddhist affirmation. No problem!

For Christians, however, the idea can be problematic. Imagining that the self comes from outside a person rather than from inside, shifting in response to others rather than emanating from some inner essence, challenges Cartesian rationalism ("I think, therefore I am") and the modernist concept of the bounded self—two ideas emphasized by Western religion and philosophy. These assumptions are so central to our shared intellectual life and how we interpret religion that many people think of them as essential elements of Christianity. And Christian doctrine itself emphasizes that Christian identity is essential, unchanging, established through baptism and nourished by the sacrament of the Lord's Supper (the ritual in which the church remembers Jesus by eating consecrated bread and wine).

But we can also understand these "traditional" Christian attitudes about the self as a social consensus. They're not a reflection of the true, unchanging nature of being human; rather, we accept them, and live as if they are the only way of imagining the world, because they're handed down personally and institutionally as the best option. In this sense, receiving baptism or Eucharist, or taking Buddhist vows of refuge, doesn't create an independent or essential identity. Our religious identities come partly from social consensus.

Later, we'll consider how religious identities that emerge from relationships can also express ultimate reality. For now, can we simply imagine that the social invitations in those hospital rooms that led me to perform alternate spiritual identities— "My father is Buddhist" and "Promise you won't leave without having a word of prayer"—might have been Mystery asserting itself in the world to console suffering people?

NAVIGATING THE TERRITORY OF INHERITANCE

Adjusting our spiritual identities to reflect the people and cultures around us is only one way that spiritually fluid people navigate complex religious bonds. At least three other approaches are identified by scholars: We can keep both our feet in both camps rather than straddling cultures (that is, we can identify 100 percent with both traditions all the time). We can have a "border identity" that recognizes the multiple influences without necessarily identifying with either or any influence (in effect, recognizing religious multiplicity without identifying with any tradition). And we can place ourselves in one primary religious camp for extended periods (passing as monoreligious until we have to move to another tradition to maintain different religious bonds, connections, and relationships).[35] People tend to employ all these strategies at different times, sometimes accepting the identities that are encouraged or imposed by parents, teachers, religious leaders, and friends, and other times rejecting those identities for something that has more personal integrity.

Inheriting or receiving complex religious bonds means the tension between hiding and disclosing is present from an early age, as Sita Dookeran described. Yet people who inherit complex religious bonds often encounter Mystery more profoundly than do those who choose multiplicity or who are in the season of curiosity—in part because being spiritually fluid is so closely aligned with racial, ethnic, cultural, and family identities.

As she has become older, Sita has experienced less tension between the Hindu and Christian dimensions of her life. "When I am in certain situations, where I am calling for help, I actually will call on both," she says. "I usually will call on Jesus and Sai Baba. For me, they are all in the same place, and neither one of them is not going to come because the other one is there, you know? That's just human ego thinking."

Like Sita, people who inherit multiplicity often enter the season of ripening: spiritual practices remain important but are less prominent, suffering becomes less intense, hiding multiplicity seems less important, disclosing it less stressful, and encounters with Mystery carry increasing authority. People in the season of ripening have a stronger sense of multiplicity's benefits, and giving back to others becomes a priority. Sita remembers:

> I actually had a vision in a meditation of my mother beside Jesus—well, together. They were both so happy and at peace together, and it just gave me this message

that I would not be betraying my mother, I would not be betraying my Hindu side, I would not be betraying my Indian heritage if I accepted this call and studied to be a [Christian] minister. And that was a huge turning point and a huge relief.

I'm not denying my Indian-ness anymore. I'm proud of it. I'm not struggling to understand "Am I Hindu or Christian?" or "I'm betraying somebody." No. I know it's all one. I saw my mom with Jesus. I know in my heart I'm everything, and that brings me a sense of peace.

FLOURISHING RECEIVED

People who inherit or receive complex religious bonds stress the benefits, not the drawbacks, of multiplicity. Their suffering, especially suffering that involves identity, loyalty, and cultural privilege, is real. But the suffering does not erase the advantages that come from owning both sides of their heritages, integrating diverse commitments and worldviews, and using their lives to address legacies of colonialism, racism, and immigration. Complex religious bonds nurture a personal, familial, communal, and spiritual integrity, creating a type of balance not available in other ways. "It's just all part of, I think, God's big plan to just bring balance back," Sita says. "That's what I was told in my meditation. I am supposed to be part of bringing the balance back, and the way I understand that is the balance that we lost through the British Empire and the oppression of these other cultures."

BEYOND INHERITANCE

Knowing that some people choose complex religious bonds and others inherit or otherwise receive these bonds expands our understanding of spiritually fluid people. It emphasizes that the social and communal influences on spirituality are minimized when we emphasize individual choice as a pathway to a spiritually fluid life.

But highlighting a social or relational pathway creates another problem. Such a pathway to complex religious bonds suggests that spirituality is primarily a human product, the result of histories and social influences in the mundane world. Putting human relationships at the center of how we form our spiritual lives minimizes the power of individual choice and *fails to account for the role of ultimate realities*—Mystery—in persuading people to nurture complex religious bonds.

So we have a conundrum. Neither the social pathway nor the cognitive pathway, together or alone, sufficiently explains how people claim and are by claimed by more than one religious tradition at the same time. To appreciate how and why people become spiritually fluid, we need a more complex account of complex religious bonds. My research suggests a third pathway: collaboration initiated by Mystery.

CHAPTER FOUR

Collaborating

N THE DAYS following the 9/11 attacks in New York City, Carlos Alejandro staffed the temporary morgue at Ground Zero and offered care to firefighters, medics, and other first responders. As a board-certified chaplain volunteering his time and expertise, he felt useful. The work was meaningful. But theologically and existentially, Carlos couldn't make sense of the disaster. The destruction, the clouds of ash, the grief: it all felt apocalyptic. Even after a decade as an ordained minister, Carlos found his religion inadequate for making sense of the violence and suffering.

"I couldn't make meaning of what was happening within the Christian paradigm," he remembers. "For me, it didn't work. When I looked for God, I couldn't find the divine—except when I felt the wind blow. In the midst of all that, I actually felt the presence of the orishas."

Orishas, deities of the African traditional religion of the Yoruba people and New World religions like Spiritism and Santeria, govern particular aspects of life. At Ground Zero, a sudden wind signaled the presence of Oya, the deity who oversees the winds of change and serves as guardian of the cemetery (and by extension, the morgue). In an instant, Ground Zero ceased to overwhelm, and Carlos remembered the spirituality he had learned from his Puerto Rican immigrant family.

"It blew me away," he says. "For me to be in Ground Zero and experiencing that energy of Oya out of the blue—because I had separated from these traditions for so many years—that blew me away. And that began my journey back to these traditions; it was post-9/11, trying to seek meaning and understanding of what was going on."

People in crisis often return to the ideas and images of their childhood religion; early spiritualities provide comfort and a way to make sense of overwhelming experiences. But for Carlos, the wind of Oya wasn't a means of coping; it was an invitation: the orishas hadn't abandoned him, and they wanted him back. His family practiced both Catholicism and Santeria, but as a child, he had learned to hide his connections to traditional African religion. As an adult, he became monoreligious; spiritual monogamy seemed necessary to serve authentically as a Protestant Christian pastor. But now, late in life, Carlos felt Mystery calling him back to complex religious bonds—an intentional, life-giving, and public collaboration with the sacred. It wasn't easy.

"I struggled for many years," Carlos says. "If I practiced, if I returned to these traditions, is it a betrayal of Christ? Am I betraying that experience I had with Jesus? It took years of my life really working through that and giving myself permission that I used to give patients who were dying—to be all of who they were, to access all of their spiritual resources. . . . I finally gave myself that permission. That part of my reality and my truth is that I walk in a world of spirits, that the orisha are for me very real."

In time, Carlos traveled to Osogbo, Nigeria, and was ordained as an Ifá priest while maintaining his credentials as a Christian pastor. "It took years of work," he says. "It took a lot of pain. There were a lot of tears and a lot of suffering in terms of being able to come out openly. I remember when I first identified as an Ifá priest publicly, my voice breaking, my voice shook

. . . and the words, the words were getting stuck in my throat. That's how bad it was."

In some ways, Carlos inherited complex religious bonds from his family and his culture, choosing to affirm them later in life. Yet in many ways, his dual affiliation with Ifá and Christianity doesn't represent personal choice or family inheritance. It's a response to the divine, a willing collaboration with Mystery.

THE COLLABORATIVE PATH

Sometimes, complex religious bonds emerge as a faithful response to God—the invitation, seduction, lure, impulse of Mystery—rather than by choice or through inheritance. It's as if the holy chooses some people for a collaborative project that requires complex religious bonds. When Mystery calls in this way, spirituality becomes an identity-in-process, mirroring experiences of the holy—experiences beyond words and gestures, logic and thought. Mystery exceeds human categories, including the categories of religious doctrine and rules.[1]

It's difficult to describe the collaborative pathway and its followers, because language can only approximate the experience. People on the collaborative pathway don't so much enter into diverse traditions or become fluent in different spiritualities as they embody multiple religious possibilities. Rather than "stepping into" or "understanding" particular religious traditions, they participate in spiritual realities that engage them. People on the collaborative path are claimed by Mystery in ways that require multiple religious and spiritual expressions.

Like Carlos, some people on the collaborative path might try to live a monoreligious life for a while; others wish that their spiritual lives were simpler and more ordinary. But their spiritualties resist straightforward expression. Mystery consistently reaches out to these people, confusing religious categories and making singularity impossible.

People on the collaborative pathway, then, work with Mystery—or Mystery works through them—to manifest certain re-alities. Their spiritual lives bring a particular sound or scent or hue to the world, one that couldn't exist without them. Their openness allows the divine to bring new spiritual possibilities into being. They respond to God, God responds to them, and the interaction generates a particular—and perhaps momentary—spirituality, something authentic, genuine, and full of life.

More than any other pathway, collaboration relies on the actions of Mystery. Yet human initiative remains central: a person's assent or acceptance matters as a necessary but insufficient catalyst. On the collaborative pathway, human action alone cannot create complex religious bonds. Mystery must participate too. Thus, the pathway relies on a dynamic interplay of divine and human energies. Mystery doesn't force or insist that people become spiritually fluid, but it delights—and responds—when they accept the challenge.

People on the collaborative path are neither nomads, crossing from one religious tradition to another, nor hybrids, whose spiritual lives result from the interaction of inherited religious cultures. They are creators, participating in an emergent multiplicity as a faithful and authentic response to Mystery. Intellect or social influences might initially draw them to multiplicity, but in time their complex religious bonds exceed human influence. It's as if they see and respond to realities hidden to others. I think of their spiritual perception as something beyond what ordinary people sense, the same way a dog smells and hears things we cannot, elephants communicate at sound frequencies below human awareness, and shrimp see more colors than humans do.[2]

Collaborating with Mystery isn't primarily an intellectual or a social process, but is participatory and intuitive. People who collaborate on complex religious bonds embody and perform spiritual possibilities at the prompting of Mystery. Yes, they draw from the religious resources learned about and received in their daily lives, from racial and family memory, and through contemplative insight. But the collaborative pathway also requires knowledge and awareness not accessible to most of us but received as a gift from Mystery itself.

CHOSEN AND FORMED FOR MULTIPLICITY

As a Buddhist priest, the man who calls himself VG oversees a congregation, leads contemplative retreats, and teaches students how to comfort others with the dharma. Seeing him at Starbucks or on the city bus, you probably would not know he is a lama—or that he is a former Christian monastic and army therapist who worships weekly at a Jewish synagogue and keeps human skulls on a tantric altar in his home. He seldom talks about his multiplicity.

"My religious experience, I cannot, I don't know, I cannot communicate that," he says. "I would like a more simple life, a life like—you know—'the herd.' You know: what everyone does.... I cannot communicate to people fully my experience.... I try my very best to communicate. And no one gets me."

VG didn't choose spiritual fluidity. It chose him, generations ago, and his great-grandmother groomed him to preserve the family vocation.

"There were always spiritual practitioners in my mother's family ... for generations before ...," he says. "It was not chosen. But I do know it was manufactured. This I know: my childhood, my great-grandmother, planned it.... She chose even before I was born. She chose. I knew this only in my late thirties or forties. I knew. I suddenly realized, 'Oh. She planned this all along.' ... It was not choice. I was beaten by life into cooperation with it."

VG grew up in Singapore in the 1970s. When he was very young, his great-grandmother removed him from his parents' home to live with her. He grew up in her village, where she raised him in isolation and took pains to introduce him to multiple religions: "She would take us to pray at the Muslim shrine on Thursday. On Friday, we go to some other shrine, and on Saturday, we go to a Hindu shrine. And on Sunday, my parents took me to church. . . . It goes like that every week. . . . So I grew up with this multiple tradition. I don't participate as a guest. I participate as a full member."

VG's great-grandmother was a tantric Buddhist shaman and animist. She meditated on decaying corpses, used Arabic words from mystic Islam to explain Buddhist doctrine, and communicated with ancestors, gods, and spirits through complex daily rituals. Some villagers bowed to her out of respect; others, out of fear: the old woman could control the weather (useful for soccer games and harvests); watered plants with fish blood to control the (potentially harmful) spirits in her garden; and dried lizards, tree frogs, puffer fish, and other creepy-crawlies under her bed to make poison. She could cast a spell to shrink a man's penis if he crossed her.

Neighbors made offerings to VG's great-grandmother, seeking her advice and healing energies. She had the power to curse or bless, and she never seemed to take a break from hosting religious ceremonies and the ongoing preparation they required.

She constantly honed VG's spiritual sensitivities. He helped prepare for rituals and, in play, chanted mantras with his stuffed animals and prepared Tibetan tantric feasts for them. He absorbed Catholic traditions from his family, his school, and Christian worship. "I always was ritually minded," he says. "I remember my grandmother telling her sister, when I wanted to make a Catholic altar [at home] . . . , 'No, we never did anything to him, and he's still being—he's behaving like one of us, like our family.' "

Family legend holds that this spiritual destiny began during the Ming dynasty. An ancestor on his mother's side, a Chinese merchant, was raped by a *phi*, a spirit, and the spirit bore him a child. Since then, all members of VG's maternal family have claimed divine ancestry, which is passed down biologically. At least one person in each generation exhibits supernatural powers. The family's spiritual patron is the Hindu goddess Kali, who wears a necklace of skulls and a skirt of arms and holds a knife dripping with blood.

But these weren't the only religious influences on VG. His parents sent him to Christian schools, took him to church weekly, and considered him a Catholic despite the multireligious influences from his great-grandmother. He experienced a profound mystical unity after his First Holy Communion in elementary school: "I felt like one with the universe and everything," he remembers. "It was like a light that joined with a bigger light. Everything was filled with light, you know—light and happiness. There was no more 'me.' No more me, no more other people, no more church, no more priest, no more nothing . . . just light."

VG's paternal grandparents were Egyptian Jews who fled to Singapore in 1932 for complex political, religious, and personal reasons. They had converted to Catholicism later in life; even so, they lit the Shabbat lamp weekly, and VG's grandfather prayed three times daily and always touched the doorpost and kissed his fingers when entering or leaving the house—like Jews touching the Torah-inscribed mezuzah that hangs at the entrance to a house.

He describes his spirituality with an analogy from Reb Zalman, a founder of the Jewish Renewal movement and a thinker profoundly influenced by Christian, Sufi, and nondual mysticisms. "Different religious traditions are different organs in one human body," VG says. "And these different pieces need to cooperate to make a single human experience. . . . There is still unity. There is unity, but there is also difference. Both are important. The unity part is that all religions are spiritual journeys, and all religions are different spiritual journeys. It's true."

I have yet to meet another person whose fluidity was "manu-factured," by family or culture, to the extreme of VG's. Yet he insists that his multiplicity wasn't entirely his great-grandmoth-er's choice. After her death, she continued to teach him through dreams and visions, communicating that she and VG—and oth-ers—are spiritually fluid because Mystery expects it; their task is to cooperate, and in cooperating, to allow the divine to manifest itself.

"I think we need to cooperate to make the experience of the divine for us," VG says. "I don't think there's a divine 'out there.' I think we make the divine. It comes from the best of us."

As they become increasingly sensitive to Mystery, even people who initially choose spiritual fluidity can shift to collaboration. It bears repeating that spiritual fluidity's seasons, experiences, and pathways aren't mutually exclusive. For example, I think of my complex religious bonds as chosen, but they still have social and collaborative dimensions. In fact, the way Mystery engaged me during a hike could be a case study of collaborative spiritual experience.

TOUCHING GROUND IN EVEY CANYON

Nothing convinces me of the truth of Buddhism's First Noble Truth (*dukkha*, suffering, the impossibility of satisfaction) like the act of writing does.[3] Once, at a coffee shop, I rewrote a single sentence for an hour or more. The argument refused to advance. Words bounced against my skull. I just *knew* my efforts dis-honored the material. Nothing worked. And then the mountain spoke, calling me from the north. I left the café.

Ten minutes later, I was hiking up Evey Canyon in the foot-hills of Mount Baldy in Southern California. As I walked among the old-growth oaks beside a spring-fed stream, the noisy con-cepts in my head dropped away, and I returned to my body: footsteps, breath, sunlight on skin, vivid blue sky, scent of sage, croaking of ravens. Anxiety evaporated. I became present to the world.

I didn't pray or engage in Buddhist practice; I simply walked until I felt grounded, present to, and engaged by the world in a way I had not been all morning. Then I sat beside the trail, above the stream, and folded my legs in the half-lotus position. I did not decide, at a conscious level, to meditate; sometimes *vipassana*—insight meditation—just happens. I sat mindfully in the forest, aware of my breathing, and noticed what was going on. That's all. (As the slogan says, "Buddhist meditation is not what you think!") My awareness flickered between an immediate nondualism, in which there was no separation between me and the canyon, and *heart knowledge*, a sense that something other than my "self" was the source of my experience and was, at the same time, knowing the experience with and through me.[4]

In time, gratitude appeared. Typically, a *vipassana* practitioner observes a mental event like gratitude, noticing the way it comes and goes. But instead of observing gratitude that morning, I engaged with it as an appropriate response to the liberation I experienced. Thus, gratitude served as an invitation, a gateway or hyperlink to a different spiritual practice. I moved into discursive meditation on creation, a Christian reflection on the Buddhist doctrine of *paticca samuppada*, "interbeing." I acknowledged how the being of the mountain, stream, trees, and sky gave rise to and sustained my own being. The experience was like living a wordless psalm or canticle, a rich appreciation of the dance of creation, the mutual indwelling, interpenetration, or abiding of all things.

But sounds from up the canyon interrupted me. Two hikers came down the trail from Potato Mountain, and the moment I heard them, I anticipated feeling angry about the intrusion. But instead of anger, I felt anticipation. I turned my head to greet them, but they were so engrossed in conversation they didn't notice me sitting beside the trail. When I realized they had not seen me, I expected to feel smug superiority; unlike me, they were in the wilderness but not present to it. But rather than judgment, I felt compassion bubble up. I noted it and returned to mindful sitting.

I couldn't have described the shift so neatly then, but in retrospect, it seems as if Christian identity faded into the background as Buddhist identity returned to the fore.

Normally, the presence of compassion would be a cue to close the meditation by sending loving-kindness to all beings and sharing with them any merit gained through the meditation practice. Instead, my imagination presented a glimpse of the praise team from a former Christian congregation. In my mind's eye and ear, Doris, John, Johnny, and Kimberly were singing "How Great Thou Art" accompanied by guitar and fiddle, and there in the canyon, I joined in (as silly as it felt). Music is not usually a part of my private spirituality; even in congregational worship, I experience it as distraction, a disruption of silence. Yet here I was in Evey Canyon on a Friday morning, singing "How Great Thou Art" to an audience of willows, ravens, and rushing water. My practice was uniquely Christian at that moment.

After the hymn, I sat in silence, listening, before hiking back to my car. At home, I drank a glass of tap water. The water in the glass had journeyed to our faucet from San Antonio Creek; it contained the stream in Evey Canyon, the rainwater washed down from mountain slopes, and the Los Angeles pollutants that threaten the San Gabriel Mountains and my own body. All of it was filtered through desert sand. I was literally swallowing the mountain, the clouds, the dew, the minerals, and the toxins. They sustained and nourished my body just as the mountain renewed my being.

During that time in the canyon, was my spirituality—was I—Buddhist, Christian, or something else altogether?

MAKING SENSE OF COLLABORATIVE SPIRITUALITY

I would say that during my visit to the canyon, I oscillated between spiritual identities and practices: from Buddhist to Christian to Buddhist to Christian. Each movement was distinct, but there was no sense of shifting from one aspect of myself to another; I felt whole, unified: two natures in one being, as it were. Many Buddhist-Christians describe this type of unity in diversity, even when one tradition takes precedence. Although the traditions are separate, they are symbiotic; each sustains the integrity of the other through a mutually supportive relationship.[5]

At times, this mutual support has less to do with a practitioner's choice than with the person's responses to subtle, interior movements, as during my experience in Evey Canyon. Spiritual identities called forth in these ways might not be real in an objective sense. Nor are they entirely subjective. They are cocreated between humans and Spirit in connection with each other. (The term *Spirit* here denotes, in the words of psychologist Jorge N. Ferrer, "an emergent creative potential of life, nature or reality."[6]) Spiritual experience emerges as a person collaborates with the ways Mystery chooses to manifest itself in the mundane world. Human contexts, language, embodiment, and faculties make a difference, yet the spiritual worlds we are calling *Mystery* are real, creative, and valuable.

If some people are spiritually fluid because they collaborate with Mystery in this sense, maybe it's natural that many Buddhist-Christian practitioners can distinguish their Buddhist and Christian dimensions yet describe themselves as Buddhist and Christian at the same time rather than as alternating between identities. They don't fluctuate from Buddhist to Christian to Buddhist, but embody both simultaneously. The "truths" of doctrine or philosophy aren't ultimate or privileged, but function as important voices in a wide-ranging conversation they are having with Mystery.

This type of collaboration isn't primarily cognitive, social, or doctrinal. It draws on broader, more holistic, and embodied ways of knowing. Instead of privileging thought, empirical evidence, and logic, it relies on intuition, imagination, empathy, beauty, meditation, contemplation, ethical impulses, and awareness of the body. The way a person collaborates with Mystery cannot be a universal human norm or an essential part of who they are. It's a manifestation in the moment, performed in the world. "We give expression to truth not by representing inwardly an outward reality," Ferrer writes with his coauthor Jacob H. Sherman, "but through our creative responses in word and deed to the pressure of a transcendent and immanent mystery and the creation it continually bestows."[7]

From this perspective, my evolving reverie in Evey Canyon could be seen as a dialogue between spiritualities shaped by my history and invitations from Mystery, Spirit, or sacred reality or realities. I knew Mystery's presence through embodied, intuitive, cognitive, and meditative sources; our conversation called me to various spiritual practices and identities, shaped by the Buddhist and Christian traditions that I know, the primary possibilities available to me in those moments. Each time I collaborated with Spirit, it responded, calling forth something new. For me the experience was less a sudden switching of gears, jolting from one framework to another, than a playful rolling with the waves—the way kayakers joyfully respond to a river's current, trusting that the boat's buoyancy will keep them afloat. Seen in this way, spiritual experience becomes "an event of vulnerable relationality—an event, therefore, of nearly inevitable transformation."[8]

We can therefore frame some spiritual identities and experiences as collaboration—a communion of knowing and being—where human wisdom, cultural context, and the creative power of Mystery flow together. With this view, we can create new possibilities for understanding spiritually fluid people, opening a dialogue less constrained by the limited doctrinal, philosophical, and human tensions that often arise.

NAVIGATING AND FLOURISHING
ON THE COLLABORATIVE PATH

Life on the collaborative pathway largely resembles choosing or inheriting complex religious bonds, with one major difference: people on the collaborative path cannot easily reject or end their spiritual fluidity to become (or pass as) monoreligious. Their spiritual fluidity functions as "a calling, a compulsion, a necessity, a survival, a means to being whole."[9] It becomes their vocation, the work they do to serve the world, and as such, it is "a special call to holiness . . . a gift to be received in fear and trembling and in gratitude and joy."[10] Jacques Dupuis describes it as a "hard asceticism" that enriches spiritual practice, purifies religious assumptions, destroys prejudices, and deepens perception of Mystery and commitment to it.[11]

On the pathway of collaboration, dwelling creatively as a spiritually fluid person can be a lifelong project, a work of performance art, a gift to the world.

CHAPTER FIVE

A Field Guide
to Spiritual Fluidity

P EOPLE WHO STRADDLE religious boundaries are difficult to identify, but we brush against them all the time.
Consider the coffee shop where I begin my day. A basketball
scout sips coffee near the window, reading the *Dhammapada*,
an early Buddhist text. He considers himself both Catholic and
metaphysical. Nearby, a Chinese Buddhist nun hangs a poster on
the community bulletin board. She's confident that Confucianism and Taoism infuse her Mahayana spirituality. At another
table, a black Christian minister confers with someone; at home,
she maintains an ancestral altar and adapts African traditional
religious rituals for her own devotions.[1] At the counter, a geneti-
cist grabs coffee for her commute. She is Christian; her husband,
Buddhist; their children, both. At the bar, a Muslim scans email.
On weekends, she joins indigenous healing rituals led by Central
American shamans and Yoruba priests. When I look around the
room, I wonder, What's the ecology, the natural history, of this
group of spiritually fluid people? What do they have in common
as individuals treading multiple spiritual paths?

Being spiritually fluid isn't a static or generic state; its roles
and functions constantly shift, and the histories, geographic locations, and languages of spiritually fluid people reflect their situations. Yet similarities, shared experiences, and mutual concerns
span different locations. Spiritual practices, for example, suf-
fuse people's accounts of complex religious bonds. So do stories

about suffering, hiding, and encountering Mystery (however it is named). Many spiritually fluid people find multiplicity beneficial. Some give back to their communities by mentoring others and sharing wisdom they discovered by living with complex religious bonds. In addition to these lived experiences, written accounts of religious multiplicity, historical and contemporary, can help identify other key features, clarify terms, and establish a descriptive taxonomy more inclusive than terms drawn from particular religious traditions.

This chapter functions as a field guide to religious multiplicity. Biologists, ecologists, and others carry field guides into the wild, where objects and phenomena naturally exist, to help identify what they're seeing. Field guides aren't comprehensive, but they make expertise portable and accessible so that we can learn to see in new ways and increase our knowledge. We become familiar with the markings and behaviors of distinct stages of development. We learn about regional differences, as well as things that are the same no matter what. A field guide develops our capacities for observation and identification so that we can eventually rely less on the book and more on our internalized learning.

SEASONS OF MULTIPLICITY

Complex religious bonds shift and morph over a lifetime, ebbing and flowing alongside the rest of the multiverse. Yet spiritually fluid people move through at least four recognizable seasons: curiosity, engagement, ripening, and generativity. Each season brings certain experiences to the fore as others fade or disappear in response to changing priorities and more-nuanced understandings. People who choose multiplicity or accept Mystery's invitation to collaborate tend to begin in curiosity, progress to engagement, and sometimes proceed to ripening and generativity. People who receive or inherit complex religious bonds tend not to experience a season of curiosity; they are born into engagement and sometimes proceed to ripening and generativity. Many spiritually fluid people spend most of their lives in one season or two, but others experience all four.

CURIOSITY

Many spiritually fluid people—especially those who choose multiplicity—begin in the season of curiosity. Spiritual practices are usually the gateway: meditation, sacred texts, prayer, ritual, justice work, and teachers generate energy, joy, and a desire to know and do more. Marie Romo, for example, first adopted yogic breathing to strengthen her lungs. She could have stopped there, but curiosity prompted her to engage with the sacred texts of Hinduism. This engagement led to other Hindu practices, which led to formal study with her swami. Ruben Habito entered the world of complex religious bonds through intellectual curiosity and then by practicing Zen meditation. Eventually he was ordained as a priest.

People in the season of curiosity are drawn to a practice, an idea, or even the ethos of an unfamiliar religious tradition. They flirt with it, testing its fit with their disposition and spiritual affinities, social and cultural situations, and sense of identity. They're not ready to identify as spiritually fluid, and they don't belong to more than one religious tradition or community; the experience is more akin to flirting than to making a commitment. They read books, watch videos, explore different forms of worship. Like people infatuated with a new friend or lover, they experience delight, freedom, newness, and insight. Some say experimenting with an unfamiliar religion feels foreign, exotic, or transgressive; they enjoy and call attention to it the way the singer Madonna's wrist once sported the red string of kabalistic Judaism. Others in the season of curiosity feel anxious. They try to keep their explorations secret, and their curiosity can feel like a shameful transgression. "It is particularly hard," one woman says, "when someone wants an explanation—something that is hard to do when you yourself aren't sure why or don't have the vocabulary to put it into words." But suffering in the season of curiosity seems minimal compared with the season of engagement.

ENGAGEMENT

People enter the season of engagement when they choose (consciously or otherwise) to nurture, adopt, or accept a spiritually fluid practice, as Marie and Ruben did. Others, like Sita and VG, are born into engagement when they inherit multiple traditions. No matter what pathway they follow into multiplicity, most spiritually fluid people spend most of their lives in the season of engagement. They deepen their sense of fluid identity, and they might engage in multiple religious communities.

People in the season of engagement weave multiple traditions into their lives. They engage in spiritual practices to one degree or another, observe multiple holidays, participate in multiple rituals with family and broader communities, and teach their children about each set of traditions. They use complex religious bonds to maintain and strengthen ties to families, cultures, and ethnic groups; solidify and celebrate aspects of identity denied or marginalized by the dominant culture; and encounter Mystery from a variety of perspectives.

Yet suffering increases during engagement. As complex religious bonds grow stronger, the stakes are higher, especially when those bonds are tied intimately to identity, family, and community. If others reject the possibility, coherence, or legitimacy of spiritually fluid lives—Marie's mother, for example, calls her spirituality "of the devil"—it can lead to separation and isolation. Deciding whether to hide or disclose multiplicity consumes much energy, as Sita and Miguel De La Torre note; discerning when and where disclosure is safe or unsafe is like constant background noise. Many who inherit complex religious bonds spend their lives in this tension.

RIPENING AND GENERATIVITY

When spiritually fluid people can claim multiplicity with confidence, framing it as a gift and not a liability, they have entered the season of ripening. Suffering eases, especially as secrecy becomes less important and disclosure less stressful. In my experience, people on the collaborative path enter this season most often, becoming elders and mentors, ancestors and guides to other spiritually fluid people. They frequently share what they've learned and experienced, and they seek to deepen and expand people's understanding of both single traditions and spiritually fluid lives. In this way, their sharing benefits both spiritually fluid people and monoreligious people.

People in the season of ripening feel less torn between communities and less concerned about demonstrating that their spirituality is normal. Helping others understand what it's like to live a spiritually fluid life becomes a priority and responsibility. At the same time, the benefits of spiritual fluidity become clearer and more familiar. People in the season of ripening hone their sensitivities to the presence and action of Mystery beyond formal spiritual practices and occasions, cultivating, encountering, and understanding Mystery in richer and more complex ways. This growth provides more-nuanced ways of understanding and articulating their experiences as spiritually fluid people. Giving back to the community—helping others who are (or are becoming) spiritually fluid—becomes increasingly important.

The season of generativity arrives through a concern for guiding and mentoring people new to complex religious bonds. Contributing to the next generation becomes a central concern during generativity, and giving back to the community becomes a central practice—as when Ruben honors his desire to interpret Christian creeds and doctrines in fresh ways informed by Zen practice. In the season of generativity, suffering related to multiplicity evaporates; hiding complex religious bonds rarely feels necessary, as community engagement and formation take more and more time and energy.

Spiritual practices remain important during both ripening and generativity, but their purposes shift. Rather than helping religiously multiple people understand and master the foundations of their traditions, spiritual practices in later seasons maintain and fine-tune the spiritual life, facilitating a relationship with Mystery. Meditation, chanting, ritual, communal worship, dance, and other spiritual practices function as a call and response to the divine, in the process enacting and creating spiritual realities. Practices don't just express, transmit, or reinforce knowledge of the divine; they become the spaces where Mystery itself is encountered and grasped.[2]

Identity becomes clearer. People in the seasons of ripening and generativity move beyond knowledge, practice, and participation to make complex religious bonds a part of who they are in relation to Mystery. They tend to identify as spiritual hybrids, multiple religious belongers, or members of multiple religious communities, and their relationship to Mystery becomes a primary focus of their daily lives.

FIVE IMPORTANT LESSONS

The seasons of multiplicity reveal the nuances of spiritually fluid lives through time. But some facets of multiplicity are constant, no matter what season people are in or what pathway they've taken to a complex religious bond. I'm not an expert on other people's experiences, but I've spent a lot of time with spiritually fluid people. They have taught me five important things about living with complex religious bonds:

IT ISN'T EASY BEING HYPHENATED

Spiritual fluidity involves family, social, political, communal, institutional, economic, and spiritual risks. It can mean being erased or silenced by people and institutions that stand at the center of things. Spiritually fluid people learn to exist at the edges of communities, where multiplicity isn't noticed and doesn't threaten the status quo. Making choices about hiding or disclosing multiplicity requires lifelong attention. At the same time, multiplicity brings a particular joy that monoreligious people don't always understand.

MULTIPLICITY IS MORE COMPLICATED THAN YOU THINK
A kaleidoscope of influences shapes spiritual fluidity, which pulsates in a matrix of decisions, priorities, benefits, strengths, problems, impacts, needs, and concerns. Multiplicity looks different at different stages of life and in different settings, and it betrays simple description or explanation. Just when you think you comprehend it, it shifts again or reveals something you never imagined. The complexity of religious multiplicity surprises spiritually fluid people as much as it surprises the monoreligious.

SALVATION IS YOUR AGENDA, NOT OURS
Christian categories like sin, salvation, idolatry, and orthodoxy aren't sufficient for talking about religious multiplicity. Complex religious bonds aren't primarily doctrinal and logical, but are embodied, relational, performed. We need shared ways of talking about what's at stake. But those approaches shouldn't privilege Judeo-Christian norms and assumptions.

WHAT YOU CALL US MATTERS
Terms like *multiple religious belonging* and *hyphenated identity* can't capture the fullness of complex religious bonds, which reflect a continuum of attractions, behaviors, and identities. We need a shared vocabulary to talk about that range of experiences. We also need (1) criteria for discerning what types of religious multiplicity shape particular people and (2) guidelines for negotiating boundaries and commitments in the midst of diverse religious and spiritual traditions and communities.

SPIRITUAL FLUIDITY ISN'T JUST
(OR EVEN PRIMARILY) A CHOICE
Multiple pathways lead to religious multiplicity, and some-times they overlap. Choice exists, but few spiritually fluid people choose their way of being religious (although they make choices about practicing or disclosing their multiplicity). People inherit religious multiplicity or accept Mystery's invitation to collabo-rate in spiritually fluid ways. Pathways other than choice play a greater role than we've tended to recognize.

UNPACKING THE FIVE LESSONS

These five lessons overlap, influencing each other in a holistic experience. But separating them allows me to flesh out distinct dimensions of spiritually fluid life. Here's what I've learned in more detail and why I think it matters. If I explain it well, spiri-tually fluid people will recognize themselves in my descriptions. That's one way to test the accuracy of my observations.

HYPHENATION ISN'T EASY
People with "hyphenated" identities claim (or are claimed by) two or more nations, races, communities, or social categories. Think of Muslim Americans, Anglo-Indians, Turkish Austra-lians, and Afro-Caribbeans, for example. Hyphenated identi-ties resonate especially with immigrants and the children of immigrants, refugee communities, and people who grow up in a current or former colony of another nation. Loyalty anchors both sides of the hyphen—loyalty to cultures, relationships, practices, nations, and landscapes. Pastor Joyce Shin calls hy-phenation "an interior landscape that consists of loyalties and commitments that sometimes overlap and other times compete with one another."[3]

Not all spiritually fluid people consider themselves hyphen-ated, and I don't want to suggest that they do or should. The idea of hyphenation, as I'm using it here, simply signals what it's like to have two or more identities wrestling in self-understanding and/or how you're understood by others. Each side of the hyphen pulls identity taut, and the tension prevents separation or isolation. Hyphenation isn't an either-or issue. It is a both-and concern. How people experience hyphenation matters most. "I felt intense pressure to be two things, approved of on either side of the hyphen," writes Indian American author Jhumpa Lahiri. "Looking back, I see that this [approval] was generally the case. But my perception as a young girl was that I fell short at both ends, shuttling between two dimensions that had nothing to do with each other. . . . In spite of the first lessons of arithmetic, one plus one did not equal two but zero, my conflicting selves always canceling each other out."[4]

Can you imagine one part of your identity canceling another many times a day? That cancellation, the tension of the hyphen, shapes a person's inner world, family relationships, self-understanding, and existential experiences. It also creates social, political, communal, institutional, economic, and spiritual opportunities and barriers. Despite the occasional social or institutional advantages of multiplicity, it can be more advantageous to pass as a nonhyphenated or singular person, especially for those religiously multiple people who rarely stand in the spotlight or identify publicly. Spiritually fluid people learn to accept the edges of communities, where their multiplicity isn't noticed and therefore doesn't threaten the status quo.

Managing the risks, tensions, opportunities, and other possibilities of religious multiplicity takes energy. People tend to use three strategies.[5] First, in some situations, they might pass as monoreligious or spiritually singular, the way a light-skinned African American at one point in history might have passed as white at work or school, or a queer athlete might pass as straight in the locker room. You might never guess that people

are spiritually fluid if they choose to pass in the places you encounter them. A Jubu at synagogue, for example, usually doesn't
tell the rabbi or other worshippers about her ongoing practice of
Tibetan Buddhist *tonglen* meditation. A Christian Yoruba practitioner doesn't correct folk in the conjuring circle when they
assume he rejects Jesus. A Hindu Christian receives Eucharist
without saying she visualizes the goddess Kali as she swallows
the bread and wine.

Why do people choose to pass? Different people do it for different reasons. Many find it simpler and more strategic to pass
(for example, as a Christian in one setting and as a Zen Buddhist or Hindu in another) than to invite questions, judgment,
and shame (or shaming) by telling others how the traditions
overlap in their families, spiritualities, identities, and religious
practices. The benefits of passing also carry a cost, however.
Passing means keeping a secret. People who pass monitor their
language, behavior, and relationships, consciously and subconsciously, to protect a hidden identity or commitment. Like a
queer person closeted from family and coworkers, spiritually
fluid people who pass are constantly hiding; they intentionally
silence a part of their lives to maintain relationships or sustain
access to the social and material goods of their families, ethnic
groups, and religious communities. This suppression can create
anxiety, cognitive dissonance, hypervigilance, and shame.

Not everyone can pass, of course, and not everyone who
can pass does so. Some people adopt a second strategy: code-
switching—shifting how they express themselves in language
and behavior to reflect or privilege one tradition or another at a
particular time. In my professional setting, for example, I code-
switch as I teach graduate students: I use Christian concepts and
metaphors with students who are training as Christian minis-
ters and chaplains, and I use Buddhist metaphors and concepts
with Buddhists, Hindus, and people who are spiritual but not

religious (SBNRs). (Similarly, another colleague uses baseball metaphors with people born in the United States and soccer metaphors with those born elsewhere!) People code-switch for a variety of reasons. They do it to signal membership in a particular social group, to show respect for a particular tradition, or to accommodate the dominant language or culture of the people around them. They also code-switch to covertly communicate with others who know both traditions and to express themselves more accurately. Paradoxically, people can also use code-switching both to stand out as not being local and to fit in. Some Christian women, for example, willingly wear a scarf when visiting a mosque; this practice is a form of behavioral code-switching. Most of us code-switch in educational settings, shifting from casual language to formal diction. Some people code-switch to pass as part of a dominant group. Switching code repeatedly in a single conversation or social setting can out you as culturally, linguistically, or religiously multiple. Spiritually fluid people who code-switch don't try to hide or silence religious multiplicity, but they might minimize one or another spiritual identity when it's useful to do so.

Code-switching implies that each religious identity is a discrete part of a person's experience, with its own vocabulary, patterns of behaving, and worldview. But many spiritually fluid people don't experience their traditions as separate; their religious bonds unite or synthesize in their experience, and they don't see their spirituality as dual or multiple but as a unified whole. They are Muslim-Christian, not people with Christian parts and Muslim parts.

Some spiritually fluid people adopt a third strategy for managing multiplicity: double consciousness. The term *double consciousness*, which appeared in the early twentieth century, was coined by W. E. B. Du Bois, an African American scholar who cofounded the National Association for the Advancement of

Colored People (NAACP). Du Bois used the term to describe living between two social realities, with allegiances to two heritages. He wrote:

> It is a peculiar sensation, this double-consciousness, this sense of always looking at one's self through the eyes of others, of measuring one's soul by the tape of a world that looks on in amused contempt and pity. One ever feels his two-ness,—an American, a Negro; two souls, two thoughts, two unreconciled strivings; two warring ideals in one dark body, whose dogged strength alone keeps it from being torn asunder.
>
> The history of the American Negro is the history of this strife—this longing to attain self-conscious manhood, to merge his double self into a better and truer self. In this merging he wishes neither of the older selves to be lost. . . . He simply wishes to make it possible for a man to be both a Negro and an American without being cursed and spit upon by his fellows, without having the doors of opportunity closed roughly in his face.[6]

Double consciousness, for Du Bois, involves tension. You are aware of your identity, goodness, morality, value, and innate capacities, and you are simultaneously aware of the negative judgments others make about your identity, goodness, morality, value, and innate capacities. You stand inside and outside at the same time. To survive—let alone thrive—you must see yourself simultaneously through your own eyes and through the eyes of others who have some measure of power in relationship to you. This bifurcated stance can be painful. Internalizing the negative definitions of others happens without awareness, and you can feel rejected—implicitly, covertly—by both communities, as if you don't belong anywhere.

Yet double consciousness also empowers, bestowing what Du Bois called the "gift of second sight." Because you live in two realities, you see things with more complexity. You are always aware of context and the ways that larger social systems shape how others perceive and receive you. You know the psyche of the dominant group as its members cannot. At the same time, you learn to decode and understand how others are seeing you. You anticipate their criticisms and micro-aggressions. You know how and when they consider you a problem. The gift of double consciousness allows you to trace the invisible commitments and values that collude to keep you in your place (as defined by more powerful people and communities). This knowledge makes it easier to resist and subvert attempts to devalue you, to keep you at the margin, and to convince you and others that you are illegitimate. Interfaith parents use the strategy of double consciousness when they teach their children that some Jewish and Christian communities may consider them not Jewish or not Christian but that those declarations do not define them. The child's both-and identities are secure, even as they are devalued in certain places.

Double consciousness can create suffering *and* freedom, joy, fulfillment, pleasure, and acute insight.[7] Hyphenated religious identities are the same way. They create opportunities and barriers, silence some people, and open new conversations for others. Spiritually fluid people can be erased, pushed to the margins, and must constantly decide whether to pass, code-switch, or simply be aware of how they're being perceived and received. Taken as a whole, these dynamics, even when positive, create psychic tensions, existential anxiety, and spiritual distress. In North Atlantic perspectives, which are dominated by monotheistic assumptions, religious multiplicity involves great ambivalence. Spiritually fluid people can love and hate their multiplicity. It feeds their souls and depletes their energies. It connects them to something greater and isolates them from others.

Religiously singular people need to acknowledge the daily struggles of spiritually fluid people, especially those struggles that emerge when personally good and life-giving experiences are publicly shamed, judged, or dismissed. If we want to be trusted enough to glimpse and understand the presence of spiritually fluid people, we need to acknowledge that it isn't easy being hyphenated. Such acknowledgment is a prerequisite to creating spaces that engage their silence, their joy, their suffering, and the gifts they offer to religion and spirituality.

IT'S COMPLICATED
Despite the challenges, religious multiplicity looks pretty simple on the surface: a person maintains bonds with more than one religious or spiritual tradition at a time, folding various beliefs, practices, and communities into a cohesive whole the way a baker folds eggs and flour and sugar together to make a cake.[8] The apparent simplicity, however, masks a tangle of influences that I sort into five interlocking categories: identity, context, affinity, expression, and disposition. No category necessarily precedes or carries more weight than does another; each constellation varies in magnitude and chronology from one spiritually fluid person to the next.

I imagine these categories as five spheres that interact with each other in various configurations—a three-dimensional Venn diagram, if you will. The spheres shrink and swell according to the seasons of a person's life. They rotate and move up and down, from side to side, and diagonally. Sometimes, two or more spheres occupy precisely the same space; other times, one sphere dominates while another, smaller one sticks out like a lump under a blanket. In some people's lives, the spheres shift constantly, forming a kaleidoscope of influences; in others, each sphere spins and vibrates in a consistent, reliable orbit. These spheres create a snapshot that helps us see the nuances and well-

trodden pathways of religious multiplicity across the landscape
of a person's life.

Each category—described below—illustrates the complexity
of each spiritually fluid life.

Identity

A person's identity shapes religious multiplicity. For example,
race and ethnicity can be the most salient aspects of identity
for some religiously multiple people, leading them to privilege
one or more religious traditions and emphasize particular types
of spiritual expression. ("What are you doing here?" a Vietnamese American teenager asked me once at a Buddhist temple.
"Buddhism is for Asians. White people worship Jesus.") Racial-
ethnic influences also shape whether a person primarily claims
an individual or a communal identity.

Other facets of identity also influence religious bonds: preferred relational styles; understanding of power and agency;
preferred ethical values and commitments; views of religion as
primarily a public or private good; and the types of personal,
communal, and religious authority that are given priority, as well
as where they are located. Identity also involves the right to name
oneself—something spiritually fluid people are often denied.

That last factor is important. Scholars work hard to establish
criteria for who is and isn't religiously multiple. A common approach is the subjective-objective criterion advocated by theologian Rose Drew and others: To qualify as a dual practitioner
or as a multiple religious belonger, a person must (1) personally
claim a dual identity and (2) be acknowledged as legitimate by
each religious community. If I claim to be Buddhist/Christian
but no Buddhist community acknowledges that I belong or at
least affirms that my belief and practice are Buddhist, then I am
not a dual practitioner.

Such distinctions are necessary for particular types of scholarship, and sometimes I make these distinctions myself. But I

generally try to honor spiritually fluid people's own naming rights—if they say they are religiously multiple, I honor this statement. I don't impose my interpretation of their commitments and experiences, but I privilege their descriptions. For example, comparative theologian Francis X. Clooney does not identify with multiple religious belonging despite his expertise in Hindu-Christian studies. I accept this identity. Buddhist practitioner and lifelong Baptist Jan Willis did not identify as Christian for a long time; now she proclaims herself "black, Buddhist, and Baptist." I also accept this identity.

Context

Religious and spiritual multiplicity emerges in particular environments. Some settings expose people to Christianity and Islam; others, to Taoism, Buddhism, and Hinduism. Some situations limit a person's exposure to religious and spiritual traditions. (For example, the neighborhood where I grew up didn't have a Buddhist temple, Jewish synagogue, or Muslim mosque; I didn't experience these as living traditions until I met practitioners in high school.) People who inherit more than one religious tradition from their parents or extended family are shaped by context, too. Some families can't expose their children to both traditions equally: a local worshipping community isn't available for one tradition, one parent considers one religion more important than the other religion, extended family or local cultures pressure families to privilege one tradition over another, and so forth. Resources matter when it comes to developing and maintaining complex religious bonds.

Context moves beyond exposure to different religions and includes many other aspects of people's lives. It includes how power flows through relationships, institutions, and social structures. It includes the resources available to teach a person about various religious traditions. Social, economic, educational, and political resources also influence a person's spiritualities, as does

a person's socioeconomic status and influence over others. Finally, various social and institutional systems in which people
live each day and perform religious and spiritual beliefs and
commitments supply other contexts for multiplicity.

Social, religious, economic, and political circumstances, especially, shape the ways that spiritually fluid people can and do
express and experience their multiplicity. In colonial Ceylon, for
example, Buddhists gained economic, social, and political influence by adding Christianity to their religious repertoire. They
would identify as monoreligious Christians in public but practice religious multiplicity at home and among extended family.
Context determines the risk involved in multiplicity, including
the likelihood of violence, shame, or ridicule and the degree
to which multiplicity is an expected part of daily life. (A child
growing up in rural Illinois, for example, might learn that religious multiplicity is sinful, whereas a child in Thailand's rural
Roi Et Province grows up expecting to practice Buddhism and
animism informed by Hindu traditions, even if those influences
aren't overtly named.) A person's circumstances create possibilities for some religious and spiritual identities, belonging, and
practices, while building barriers to others.

Affinity
Sometimes, a particular person, landscape, or idea draws us
inexplicably, like a moth to the front-porch light. We and the
person or idea fit together, and this strong sense of relationship ignores proximity or logic. I have an affinity for the desert,
for example, even though I grew up in fertile green farmlands.
Similar affinities draw us to particular religious and spiritual
traditions, leading us to claim and be claimed by them. One
tradition might seduce us intellectually, while the worship style
of another fits our exuberant physicality. (I once saw a PhD in
Christian theology dancing exuberantly during a Krishna ritual.) One religious community might speak better to our social

needs and ideals, while another feeds us emotionally, culturally, or personally. Sometimes, a religion's organizational structure lures us; some people prefer a more centralized and hierarchical institution such as Catholic Christianity, while others prefer decentralized traditions such as Hinduism. Our affinities can also push us away from some types of religious expression.

Expression
We express religious bonds and identity in various ways, and these expressions create dilemmas for spiritually fluid people. Some religions and spiritual traditions require adherents to dress in particular ways. Should a Christian Muslim cover her head during Sunday worship? Can a Buddhist Jew wear a prayer shawl during Zen meditation? Religions also have particular sacred languages (Hebrew, Pali, and Latin, among others), particular sacred texts, and specialized technical vocabularies. Should a Buddhist-Christian use a Pali prayer during a Christian meditation? When a spiritually fluid community gathers in silence, are the participants praying, contemplating, or meditating? Is it fair to interpret the Christian Bible through the lens of Mahayana Buddhist doctrine? Certain symbols, objects, and rituals are central to various religions. Should a Yoruba Christian receive the Eucharist? Can a Hindu Christian include an image of Jesus on the ritual altar? What happens if a Zulu Christian sacrifices a chicken during Good Friday worship? Standard prayer styles, expected behaviors, and sacred sites all play into the choices faced by spiritually fluid people. Can a Native American medicine wheel serve as sacred space for a *santero* or *santera* Jew? Do Christian Hindus cross themselves after Hindu puja? Does a Buddhist Catholic shake hands or bow when greeting friends at church or temple? Does this person mutter *"Amido-fo"* or say "Peace be with you" at Mass during the ritual exchange of peaceful greetings? Answers to these questions depend in part on disposition.

Disposition

A person's character and the qualities of the mind and heart also shape religious multiplicity. A Jewish Muslim, for example, might find his or her intellect nourished by Judaism, while the practice of kneeling and bowing at the mosque allows the person to honor God physically in ways that spoken prayer does not. The singing at a Pueblo dance might move people emotionally in ways missing from their Buddhist practice, whereas Buddhist doctrine fits their ethical framework. Many dispositions, from contemplative to prophetic, help forge bonds with a religious or spiritual tradition. So do various experiences, from words, images, music, and movement to silence, solitude, and mystery. Spiritually fluid people sometimes take part in multiple religions because one tradition fits some of their dispositions but not all. For example, religion for some is primarily individual; for others, primarily communal. In making major decisions, people can prefer either collaboration with God or self-direction. Some take comfort in a nondual understanding of reality; others find dualism helpful. People's dispositions lead them toward or away from particular religious traditions at certain seasons of life.

Deciding where and how to disclose or claim multiplicity further complicates spiritually fluid lives. Wherever they go, spiritually fluid people decide and prioritize who should know about their multiplicity and what to reveal about it: Should my boss know I'm Hindu and Christian? Should my parents know I've been studying the Torah on Fridays while going to the gurdwara with them on weekends? Will my professor understand that I legitimately celebrate the Jewish High Holidays after I missed class last semester for Ash Wednesday worship?

In making these decisions, spiritually fluid people constantly weigh the advantages, disadvantages, and other possible outcomes in relation to family, work, vocation, spiritual communities, the wider community, and society in general.

Sometimes it's easier to pretend to be monoreligious!

• • • • •

The complexities of religious multiplicity—identity, context, affinity, disposition, and expression, as well as decisions and priorities related to context—make a difference. No spiritually fluid person's experiences match another's exactly. As a result, it's impossible to make universally accurate, general statements about spiritually fluid people as a group. It's also difficult to research, identify, or typify spiritually fluid people—one reason for so much theoretical reflection on religious multiplicity but so little empirical research.

DOES SALVATION MATTER?

For some (if not most) Christians, the issue of salvation—eternal redemption or restoration by God—is central to faith. From this perspective, humans are sinners separated from God, and each person needs God's forgiveness and acceptance to be saved and spend eternity with God after biological death. The way to receive God's forgiveness and acceptance—and for some Christians, the *only* way—is to acknowledge Jesus as lord and savior. In some forms of Christianity, Jesus, as the Messiah, mediates salvation: accept Jesus, and you'll be saved; reject Jesus, and you will be punished. This understanding, linked both to a desire for all humans to be saved and to the drive of Christian nation-states to consolidate as much political and economic dominion as possible, drove much Christian missionary effort in the nineteenth and twentieth centuries. Christianity remains the dominant and privileged religion in the United States and Europe, giving the question of salvation special significance in these cultures.

Salvation, however, isn't a concern for most religions. It's a Christian question; it makes no sense to ask a Jew, Muslim, Buddhist, or Hindu, "Are you saved?" or "Don't you worry about eternal judgment?" In these traditions, humans aren't in danger of eternal damnation; they don't need divine salvation. The metaphysics and cosmologies of these traditions don't necessarily address life after death or imagine an eternal realm where humans are united with God. These differences exist for many reasons, of course. Some religions don't have a doctrine of sin; others don't emphasize human brokenness or a need to reconcile with the divine. Making salvation a key concern in conversations about religious multiplicity means imposing a Christian concern on other religions. Debates about whether (and how) spiritually fluid people can experience Christian salvation necessarily privilege Christian doctrine, erasing the core tenets of other traditions. And salvation is tangential, if it's a concern at all, to most spiritually fluid people.

All religious traditions, of course, can and should evaluate religious multiplicity from their own perspectives. But when we begin those conversations with doctrine rather than experience, we keep spiritually fluid people at the margin rather than seeking to learn from them how and why multiplicity is a valid or preferred option. This approach frames the conversation in terms irrelevant to some spiritually fluid people and some religious traditions. Rather than asking *Aren't you worried about salvation?* or *Can spiritually fluid people be saved?*, we should ask *What can the experiences of spiritually fluid people teach us about salvation? How can those experiences correct, enrich, or expand Christian understandings of salvation?* We need humility to evaluate our (monoreligious) understanding in light of religious multiplicities.

NAMES MATTER

There's no consensus about what terms best describe religious multiplicity.[9] Some people advocate for *multiple religious belonging*, but *belonging* only works for traditions that have members, especially members of a particular local community (like Christians and Jews). Others prefer *dual religious practice*, but *practice* has two problems. It works best for traditions that emphasize particular forms of behavior over doctrine (such as ritual in Santeria, meditation among some Buddhists, and the Five Pillars of Islam for Muslims), and it emphasizes behavior without accounting for other types of religious bonds: community, identity, affiliation, heritage, and so forth.

Other terms for religious multiplicity don't emphasize membership or practice but make problematic assumptions about human nature or carry intellectual baggage that doesn't fit the worldview of many religions and spiritualities. The term *religious hybridity*, for example, implies that spiritually fluid people mix traditions to create something new; from this perspective, spiritually fluid people are not both-and, as many claim, but meld two (or more) traditions into a new and unique religious worldview. Likewise, talking about complex or multiple religious identities implies that spiritually fluid people understand their spirituality as part of their identities. Yet some spiritually fluid people call themselves SBNRs without claiming particular traditions. For traditions that begin with an assumption that there is no self, like Buddhism, the term *identity* is problematic from the beginning! Christian theologian John J. Thatamanil uses the term *participation*, saying that "multiple religious participation is the conscious (and sometimes even unconscious) use of religious ideas, practices, symbols, meditations, prayers, chants, and sensibilities drawn from the repertoires of more than one religious tradition."[10] The term captures the breadth of multiplicity but focuses too much on individuals without emphasizing communal participation.

We need to name and describe spiritually fluid people in a systematic way that doesn't privilege a particular religious tradition or set of philosophical assumptions. Although assumptions and commitments stand behind all terms, it's helpful to use language broad enough to include most expressions of religious multiplicity and nuanced enough to distinguish its types. For this reason, I have used the terms *spiritual fluidity, religious multiplicity,* and *multiple (or complex) religious bonds.*

These umbrella terms are broad enough to provide a useful, overarching category. They encompass many types of religious multiplicity—belonging, practice, identity, influence, affinity, and hybridity. The terms also describe two types of people: those who connect to a tradition but who are not recognized by "insiders" or others sharing that tradition, and those recognized by a community as "one of ours," with or without the participants' affirmation.

Still, my umbrella terms lack enough nuance to distinguish particular manifestations of religious multiplicity or to account for how multiple religious bonds shift over time. Several degrees of multiplicity cluster beneath the broad umbrella, creating a continuum of spiritually fluid people. Because these degrees aren't necessarily linear or developmental, we shouldn't expect spiritually fluid people to move sequentially from one end of the continuum to another as if they are progressing through levels of a video game. People can also move from a "softer" bond to a "firmer" bond much further along the continuum without experiencing the degrees of multiplicity in between. The figure shows how I envision that continuum.

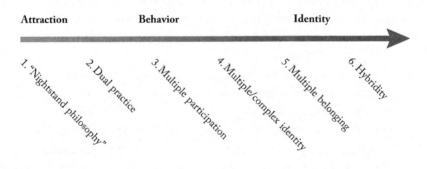

Continuum of Complex Religious Bonds (or Religious Multiplicity)

Attraction   Behavior   Identity

1. "Nightstand philosophy"
2. Dual practice
3. Multiple participation
4. Multiple/complex identity
5. Multiple belonging
6. Hybridity

A *nightstand philosopher* feels attraction—intellectual, kin-esthetic, aesthetic, geographic, relational, by disposition—to a tradition but doesn't claim to be a part of it (or possibly any tradition, for that matter).[11] These spiritually fluid people might read popular or scholarly books about religion at bedtime, try out practices such as meditation or divination, decorate with religious art, wear jewelry with religious symbols, and so forth. Usually they are flirting with a tradition; there's something in-triguing, a draw, a curiosity—perhaps even a romantic-erotic crush—but no consistent practice, participation in community, strong bond, or sense of identity. Sometimes it can be difficult to distinguish a nightstand philosopher from someone who has ap-propriated a religious culture to enhance his or her own status.

Dual practice describes spiritually fluid people who regu-larly and intentionally practice spiritual disciplines or religious behaviors from two or more traditions. They find the practices personally helpful, and there is a level of commitment or a bond to the traditions as a part of personal spirituality. At first, these practices might be solitary but can progress to practice with a community of like-minded people, a congregation, or a for-mal, institutional community. Still, dual practitioners might not identify as an adherent to all (or any) traditions. They are not consistently, intentionally committed to a formal, communal ex-pression of the religion. Their forms of practice might ebb and flow over the seasons of their lives without affecting their rela-tionships or identity. Dual practitioners might not be recognized as spiritual or religious peers or family by people born into the traditions they practice.

Multiple participation describes spiritually fluid people who engage more fully in the life of a tradition. They have moved closer to institutional expressions of their communities (such as a church, temple, or mosque). Other participants recognize them by sight, acknowledge them as more than visitors, and might consider them informal friends of the community. For example, the Christian husband of a Jewish woman might attend synagogue, participate in the weekly Sabbath ritual, and help raise the couple's children as Jews without converting or becoming a member of the synagogue. He participates in his own Christian community and his wife's Jewish community, but he identifies as Christian and belongs to a particular church congregation.

Multiple or *complex identity* signals a spiritually fluid person whose multiplicity has become a part of the individual's self-description. These people practice and participate in expressions of more than one religious tradition, seeing themselves as part of particular communities. Not only are they influenced by the traditions, but people with a complex religious identity also claim these traditions for themselves. Although both traditions don't necessarily recognize them as adherents, these people sense themselves subjectively as being committed, or having commitments, to both. Someone with a multiple or complex religious identity claims a bond to two or more traditions.

Multiple belonging signals spiritually fluid people who claim two or more traditions personally *and* who are affirmed as *co-religionists* by religious communities or by followers of each tradition. Both religious communities claim a multiple belonger, and the person claims both traditions as well. For example, Amir Hussain, a scholar of Islam at Loyola Marymount University in Los Angeles, is both Muslim and formally affiliated as an adherent of his late wife's Christian congregation in Toronto. (They married there in 1989 in an interfaith ceremony that incorporated both Muslim and Christian elements.) "While I am satisfied in my own Muslim tradition," Hussain writes, "there are parts of Christianity in general and the United Church [of Canada] in particular that speak to my soul. I love the music in Christian worship, which is absent in formal Islamic worship, but present of course in Islamic religious life. I also need the ministry of women, which again I find more fully expressed in

Christian worship than in Muslim worship. Of course, the social justice that [Trinity-St. Paul's United Church] puts into action also has deep connections with Muslim traditions. I am grateful to be one of the many members of this United Church of ours."[12] Thus, Hussain isn't Christian or Muslim-Christian, but for personal and relational reasons, he participates in the life of both Christian and Muslim communities. His religious complexity manifests as dual belonging without implying multiple identities.

Hybridity typically means mixing, the way farmers create a new type of corn by cross-pollinating two types to produce one hybrid plant that's genetically different from its parents. A mule is a hybrid of a female horse and a male donkey. Similarly, a religious hybrid no longer distinguishes between two or more traditions but mixes them to create a new spirituality—something similar to but different from the original religions.[13] Such a person is neither this nor that, but is something unique; the person manifests a spirituality or religious practice that defies the expectations of the original traditions, which are combined and transformed in the individual's being, practice, and life. Some consider Brother Ishmael Tetteh's movement, Etherean Mission, a hybrid religion. It considers itself a spiritual mission that departs from the institutional Christian church by incorporating traditional African mysticism, giving authority to the Qur'an and other sacred texts in worship and teaching, and praying not in the name of Jesus but in the name of the "Christ Love."[14]

We have many options when it comes to naming types of spiritual fluidity. I draw three conclusions from the varied nomenclature. First, *religious multiplicity* covers a broad territory—from attraction and practice to identity, membership, and belonging. Second, various degrees of multiplicity fall on a continuum but aren't linear; a person doesn't necessarily progress from one stage of multiplicity to another. Finally, because multiplicity manifests itself in diversity, spiritually fluid people must be allowed to describe themselves. They own the naming rights to their experience and identity; they know better than anyone else what they should be called and how their spirituality is best described. When we honor their naming rights, we help spiritually fluid people claim a place in a world that mostly assumes monoreligious identities and commitments. By naming themselves, they begin to move from the margins to the center, no matter how they came to claim, or be claimed by, multiple religious and spiritual traditions.

LENSES, LANGUAGES, MAPS: METAPHORS FOR LIVING WITH COMPLEX RELIGIOUS BONDS

Spiritually fluid people use at least five metaphors to name what they experience: crossing boundaries, changing religious lenses, learning new languages, following a map, and running multiple software programs with a single operating system.[15]

Some people constantly cross from one religion to another, then return. Just as travelers can immerse themselves in a different culture for a few weeks or months, people can also cross into another religion to experience it from within, then return to their home traditions with a broader vision and new ways of engaging in familiar territory. The metaphor of crossing and returning shapes the practice and theory of interfaith and interreligious dialogue, and for comparative scholars like Paul Knitter, the temporary crossing functions as a scholarly method: They cross into a tradition, describe what they see, then return to their home tradition and describe what looks similar, what looks different, and how their perspectives have changed because of their spiritual travels.

This experience of changed perspectives fits the idea that religious traditions are maps of particular territories rather than pathways to a goal. As Drew writes, "every person forges his or her own path up the mountain and no two paths are the same."[16] In this sense, a person's spiritual path is his or her actual life; the religious tradition functions as a navigation tool.

Another metaphor implies that spiritually fluid people look through two lenses, the way a nearsighted person uses a pair of eyeglasses to see at a distance or a sports fan uses binoculars to see action far down the field. For spiritually fluid people, one lens might be Muslim and another Hindu; one Buddhist, the other Christian. "Initially, these two lenses are separate," Drew writes, "and one flits back and forth between the views they respectively afford. But as, over time, one is able to focus more successfully through each lens and to make increasing sense of what one is seeing through each, these lenses begin to converge, affording a single vision of reality as seen through the area of overlap between them."[17] Drew is quick to add, however, that no matter how much comes into focus as the lenses partly overlap, the overlapping doesn't completely erase "double vision" when each lens reveals something different. Thatamanil calls this way of seeing "binocular wisdom," saying it allows him to live "a life that is all the more Christian for being Buddhist."[18]

Others use the metaphor of language to describe complex religious bonds. People born into interfaith families are religiously bilingual from birth; they grow up using vocabulary and concepts from both traditions. Some observers think it's easier for people to embrace religious multiplicity if they learn several religious languages as children. People who choose multiplicity, on the other hand, must develop facility in a second tradition; their first religion is the mother tongue, or heart language, and a second tradition provides new words, new ideas, and new ways of thinking. The more fluent a person becomes in the second tradition, "the more aware she is of things in her second language that cannot be expressed in her first, such as idioms, concepts, or subtleties of grammar," writes biblical scholar Jonathan Homrighausen. "She may rely on different languages for different purposes or associate them with different contexts: one language for home life, for family, with slang usage and emotional attachment, and another language for work life, spoken in a more formal manner and with less emotional attachment to the language."[19]

Research among Catholic Christians with bonds to Buddhism suggests that spiritual vocabularies become mixed as religious fluency increases, the way bilingual people sometimes speak Spanglish, using idiom and slang from both languages in a single sentence.[20] Sometimes, spiritually bilingual people rely on one tradition's language to describe practices and another tradition's language to describe belief. As a person becomes more fluent in both religious languages, differences become clearer. At the same time, increased fluency causes both languages to shape each other beyond typical religious structures and institutions.[21]

Finally, John Berthrong turns to metaphors of technology, suggesting that multiple religious bonds are like different software programs running in a single operating system. "I have come to believe that modern MRPers [multiple religious participants] seek to enrich and renew, but not to replace, the fundamentals of root religions," he says. From this perspective, spiritually fluid people "add programs" to their spiritual and religious computers without "tinkering with the basic operating system."[22] Thus, a person has a primary tradition that functions as their spiritual operating system, but the person can also run secondary traditions when they are useful and appropriate.

Each of these metaphors is useful to some degree. But none captures the fullness of living with spiritual fluidity. Complex religious bonds might function as a way of seeing or speaking for some; others find it more accurate to imagine primary and secondary traditions. Still others emphasize the dynamic of crossing and returning. The infinite variety of complex religious bonds can never be captured by finite human thought or speech, but I find one metaphor particularly helpful: the concept of oscillation, sweeping back and forth like a fan on the swing setting.[23]

OSCILLATION AS A NORM

The term *oscillation* describes how some spiritually fluid people shift rapidly between religious perspectives, maintaining a coherent religious identity where traditions overlap. The convergence increases over time, with an ongoing swing between similarities and differences preventing distortion. The person's preferences don't dictate how the traditions are engaged or which concepts are primary. Rather, Drew writes, *"the traditions themselves* dictate the balance: where they can agree, the Buddhist Christian should allow them to agree; where they cannot agree, the Buddhist Christian should allow them to disagree."[24]

This metaphor allows ongoing growth—or at least allows shifts—in how a spiritually fluid person engages in the traditions, singly and together. Oscillation describes my experience of shifting back and forth from Buddhist to Christian language, concepts, and practices in clinical work, in teaching, and in ministry. The convergence between the traditions becomes larger, and it best guides my action, providing a sort of spiritual or religious triangulation to measure how near (or far) I am from a "truth" that fits both the situation and each tradition without betraying the situation or either tradition. At the same time, distinctions between the traditions become more pronounced; I see them with increasing clarity and understand better why they need to be honored to protect the integrity of the traditions. Often, those differences help me see, experience, and understand religious truth in richer ways—as well as showing me where I must decide what to believe and to practice. Paying attention to belief and practice, however, isn't enough. We can only understand the experience of complex religious bonds by turning to *meaning* and *transformation*, which I discuss in chapter 6.

CONCLUSION

Spiritually fluid people live complicated lives. Their multiple bonds require an ongoing negotiation of personal, relational, and cultural factors, and this negotiation has different priorities, according to the seasons of a person's life. Spiritually fluid people shift over time from curiosity to engagement, from ripening to generativity. Understanding the risks, limits, complexities, and influences at play in spiritually fluid lives helps clarify why religious multiplicity seems exceptional. Complex religious bonds involve much more than saying yes to particular doctrines, or finding ways to reconcile conflicting beliefs, or choosing what you want from a spiritual buffet.

By now, you realize you shouldn't be seduced into thinking this book offers a clear typology, a way of diagnosing or evaluating spiritually fluid people. I'm not trying to isolate the factors that contribute to religious multiplicity or propose a preferred way of understanding it. Rather, I offer three ways to think about the primary elements of religious multiplicity as lived experience. I don't want to limit expressions of multiplicity or argue that it has only three sources. Rather, I want to tease out the interplay of human agency, social relationships, and sacred invitation to understand how all three motivate and shape spiritually fluid people.

CHAPTER SIX

Observations,
Implications,
Provocations

THIS EXPLORATION of spiritual fluidity suggests that complex religious bonds surround us, if we know how to see them. They swirl through Sita Dookeran's steamy childhood kitchen in Winnipeg as she cooks with her mom, and they nestle among VG's statues and prayer beads on his personal altar in California. They take notes in Ruben Habito's classrooms, from Japan to Texas, they reach out to suffering people at Ground Zero with Carlos Alejandro, and they sip boba at Marie Romo's favorite café. We've seen spiritually fluid people in politics and entertainment, professional sports, classrooms, and city buses. Spiritual fluidity makes itself at home in private apartments and public devotions, at funerals and weddings, in congregations, at staff meetings, at Cub Scout gatherings, and everywhere in between. Despite their frequent invisibility, the pervasiveness of complex religious bonds makes them a gentle but persistent feature of humanity, individually and in community.[1]

How, then, will spiritual fluidity influence our collective futures?

As the book closes, it's time to put my cards on the table, so to speak, and tally the influence of complex religious bonds. Accordingly, this chapter shifts from the past and present of spiritual fluidity to imagine a shared future shaped in more overt ways by complex religious bonds. Previous chapters emphasized how individuals and communities cope with, celebrate, and strategize around spiritual fluidity. Here I consider how spiritual fluidity might shape us in ways we haven't anticipated or intended. I'll also make some informed guesses about the nature of Mystery and the divine-human relationship in light of religious multiplicity. I'll start with three observations shaped by historian Peter Burke's analysis of cultural change.[2]

OBSERVATIONS

These observations aren't unique to me, and in some ways, they are quite mundane. But they shape the way I view spiritual fluidity and its influence on religious life in North America, and they inform everything I say in this chapter. First, spiritual fluidity will continue to grow. Second, the growth will be a local manifestation of global processes. And finally, spiritual fluidity will have two effects. It will, primarily, subvert and expand notions of normal spirituality. Secondarily, it will make interreligious dialogue and cooperation more complex.

INCREASING SPIRITUAL FLUIDITY

Spiritual fluidity promises to increase in the United States, not least because of immigration.[3] There are two reasons that immigration shapes spiritual fluidity. First, immigrants continue to diversify North America's religious communities. Second, recent immigrants have come primarily from places where spiritual fluidity is an expected and accepted practice.

One-quarter of new permanent residents to the United States in 2012, for example, identify as Buddhist, Hindu, Muslim, or non-Christian. They tend to be more observant of their religious traditions than are the majority population, suggesting that more US citizens are interacting more frequently with highly active participants of religious traditions other than Christianity and Judaism. Significantly, being exposed to a variety of spiritual traditions, especially through interactions close to home, seems to be a factor in choosing or inheriting complex religious bonds.

In addition, most new immigrants to the United States come from Asia, Africa, and other places where spiritual fluidity is a cultural norm. The number of US residents claiming spiritual practices that are inherently multiple—followers of folk religions from China and Hong Kong, for example, Asian Buddhist traditions that incorporate Taoist and Confucian elements, and African traditional religions—continues to rise. (In Europe, officials note that some Muslim refugees practice "strategic multiplicity" by converting to Christianity to gain access to services and resources—and religious privilege—they perceive as vital to successful relocation.) Current estimates suggest that up to 1.5 million new US residents since the beginning of the twenty-first century expect, accept, and engage in spiritually fluid practices and communities. It's likely that the spiritually fluid population of the United States already exceeds the population of Presbyterian Christians, and the growing presence of complex religious bonds seems likely to make spiritual fluidity more attractive to greater numbers of people.

As immigration leads US residents to encounter more and different religious and spiritual options, spiritual fluidity seems likely to increase. Over time, complex religious bonds may cease to be exceptional, with a critical mass of people considering them normal spirituality.

REFLECTING GLOBAL INFLUENCES

Spiritual fluidity in Europe and North America emerged historically from a confluence of colonization, trade, migration and immigration, the commodification of spirituality and religion, expanded communication networks, and globalization. Likewise, spiritual fluidity in Asia, Africa, and other locations reflects historical encounters with similar human activities. Local manifestations of spiritual fluidity, then, reflect rich, creative, and diverse understandings of religion. Specific to one ecosystem and network of relationships, these understandings are nonetheless shaped by broad historical, political, economic, and cultural forces. Complex religious bonds in Billings, Montana, look quite different from those in Nairobi, Kenya, and Zurich, Switzerland.

But local spiritual fluidity remains embedded in larger social and religious realities. No matter how idiosyncratic one person's spiritually fluid practices and understanding might be, they still reflect the influence of broader sociopolitical, economic, and historical events—both the events that precede a person's complex religious bonds and those that continue to shape new spiritual fluidities in the present and future. We should stay alert to the systemic causes and conditions that create complex religious bonds, and we should avoid framing these bonds as individual choices or relational accidents.

EXPANDING CONVENTIONAL THINKING

Most people in the United States think in conventional ways about religion and spirituality, accepting and reproducing a "normal spirituality" that assumes that religious bonds are singular, chosen, and defined by belief and belonging. Culturally, we treat religious traditions as monolithic in thought and practice—as distinct entities with clear boundaries. We believe that doctrinal differences cannot or should not be reconciled or held in tension. We want people to choose: pick one or the other.

But spiritually fluid thought and practice subvert these understandings, blurring our carefully constructed boundaries, binaries, and distinctions. Spiritually fluid people emphasize practice, culture, and relationship as much as, or more than, belief, belonging, and choice. People choose loyalty to conflicting relationships, communities, worldviews, and values rather than compromising them for the sake of religious purity. This commitment to loyalty rather than purity requires us to expand our thinking about religion: broaden the categories and shift how we understand religious commitment, belonging, belief, and practice. In the process, we revisit and revise the implicit criteria we use to judge religion and spirituality. New ways of knowing become more important than cognition, logic, and systematic doctrinal structures.

As spiritually fluid people become more visible, and as monoreligious people begin to recognize and explore their own multiplicities, spiritual fluidity will bring new complexity and texture to interreligious dialogue and interfaith cooperation. Interreligious conversations that neither include nor recognize spiritual fluidity seem increasingly insufficient, if not naive. They maintain the illusion that religious traditions are strictly segmented when, in practice, the traditions overlap. Interreligious dialogue and cooperation will increasingly need to include and address the personal and familial dimensions of religious pluralism rather than focusing on pluralism's institutional, cultural, and sociopolitical facets.

IMPLICATIONS

The preceding observations carry implications, of course. It's too soon to say which possibilities will take root and gain strength, which ones can be cultivated to bear nourishing fruit, and which might wither and die before blooming. But three potential implications of spiritual fluidity are particularly intriguing to me: First, it increasingly highlights the social and embodied dimensions of religion. Second, it contributes to human flourishing. And third, spiritual fluidity requires new norms and different criteria for engaging and assessing religious commitment and expression.[4]

These implications already shape religious life in the United States and elsewhere. Their effects so far seem implicit and largely unintentional; they deserve broader recognition so that we can engage them critically, with care and attention, in our families, communities, and institutions. How we respond to spiritual fluidity shapes the future of religion and spirituality in the United States and beyond; a curious and welcoming stance not only is preferable but also will lead to the best possible outcomes.

THE SOCIAL AND MATERIAL DIMENSIONS OF RELIGION

As more people engage in spiritually fluid thought and practice, in public and in private, complex religious bonds become more visible.[5] They show up in our families, our institutions, and our public and political life. As the visibility of these bonds increases, so does people's acceptance of them. An effect of this, I suspect, will be more attention to, and greater clarity about, the social, relational, historical, material, and performative dimensions of religion and spirituality. Decades from now, doctrine, belief, and congregational membership might no longer be a person's first associations when the topic of religion comes up; instead, relationships, meaning, and practice could become primary.

It's increasingly difficult, then, to imagine religion and spirituality as only—or primarily—a private, individual decision about what to believe or where to affiliate. Complex religious bonds are a response to how our lives are formed through an intricate dance of families, cultures, communities, and Mystery itself (or "Mysteries themselves" for polycentric pluralists). It seems to me that religion and spirituality are public and communal before they are internalized as individual or private; they are more likely to shape our inner life than to reflect or emerge from it. Spirituality comes to us from outside before it shapes our thoughts and emotions. Spiritual fluidity makes the public, communal nature of religion difficult to ignore.

Our choices and desires, then, are only part of how we become and remain spiritual. Spirituality takes root in our hearts and minds *after* it is encountered and formed by relationships, practices, and communities—all of which we experience through our bodies. Religion and spirituality are cultural, social, biological, and historical, fashioned from fabric and paper and flesh and voices, bread and wine and rice and ritual. They involve internal and personal responses to Mystery, but we receive and perform religion as much as we think and feel it. We cannot access a pure, disembodied, ahistorical religious truth; we can only receive the spirituality that manifests itself through skin and bone and text and relationships. Our bodies and our communities enable us to live in religious ways. Even the presence and action of Mystery lodge in our bodies and show up in the material world beyond mind or spirit. We embody spirituality; we don't just believe it. And spiritual fluidity illustrates this embodiment, especially through the social and collaborative pathways to complex religious bonds.

BENEFITS TO HUMAN FLOURISHING

As spiritual fluidity matures and becomes more visible, the ideas and attitudes it informs are likely to contribute more frequently and more overtly to civic life, family relationships, education, entertainment, and other human interactions. I'm convinced spiritual fluidity can advance and support human flourishing.

Research suggests that people who embody other types of multiplicity, including biracial people and "third-culture kids" (children who grow up in a country other than their parents' homeland), think and relate in more creative, flexible, and open-minded ways than does the general population.[6] They access a broader store of knowledge when faced with challenges or new information, and their perceptual skills develop earlier in life, and with more nuance, than those of people in monocultural settings. Their tribalism—rejection of social out-groups—decreases. Their in-group becomes larger. People shaped by multiplicity intuitively discern and adopt new community norms; they adapt quickly to new settings, have broader worldviews, and demonstrate greater cultural awareness. They're also less anxious in the presence of social differences, and they find it difficult to embrace or maintain rigid ideas about identity.

"The point," says writer Moises Velasquez-Manoff, "is that diversity—of one's own makeup, one's experience, of groups of people solving problems, of cities and nations—is linked to economic prosperity, greater scientific prowess and a fairer judicial process. If human groups represent a series of brains networked together, the more dissimilar these brains are in terms of life experience, the better the 'hivemind' may be at thinking around any given problem."[7] By analogy, these positive traits are likely to appear as well among spiritually fluid people and communities. While we lack empirical research to make a definitive association, the adaptive traits identified among people shaped by multiplicity mirror what spiritually fluid people describe as benefits of complex religious bonds. Spiritual fluidity compels people to act differently—socially, politically, and morally—than they would otherwise.

Significantly, the ways that spiritually fluid people talk about their lives usually reflect maturity and the life-giving qualities of personal stories identified by narrative psychologists.[8] According to psychology, the stories we tell about ourselves establish a sense of identity, expressing our values, preferences, commitments, and beliefs. Stories that promote life and satisfaction tend to include six elements, which I often see in the accounts of spiritually fluid people. Their personal narratives are coherent; credible; differentiated, in terms of identifying multiple influences on their growth; flexible; and open to engaging the world; and they demonstrate *generative imagination*, a creative turn to serving the world in ways that care for, and improve the lives of, others. Personal and communal reconciliation figure heavily among many stories of spiritual fluidity, and spiritually fluid people in the seasons of ripening and generativity particularly demonstrate *generative imagination*. Thus, the stories told by many spiritually fluid people reflect psychological health and promote flourishing.

The life-giving aspects of complex religious bonds don't

only benefit spiritually fluid people. Insights born of religious multiplicity also benefit monoreligious people by contributing to the wisdom, compassion, and transformation of monoreligious communities. When spiritual fluidity blurs the sharp lines between religious traditions, highlighting how traditions overlap and influence each other, muddying religious waters, and making spiritual and religious commitments more complex and more ambiguous, harmful religious norms are more easily dismantled. We are invited to think critically about what we believe and practice. This greater complexity creates new and generative possibilities, perhaps especially among people who are committed to a single religious tradition and yet who try to identify their own spiritual multiplicities (whether these people become spiritually fluid or not).

Spiritual fluidity's greatest gift to religion—and by extension to human flourishing—might be the accelerated shift from "*analytic* thinking that drives wedges between different parts of a whole," in the words of theologian Emmanuel Lartey, to "*synthetic* thinking and practice, which incorporates several elements into a 'gestalt' in which the whole always exceeds the sum of the parts."[9]

NORMS AND CRITERIA

As spiritual fluidity continues to grow in breadth and visibility, we will need tools for assessing whether particular expressions of this fluidity are responsible, have integrity, contribute to human flourishing, and sufficiently honor the traditions brought together. A mash-up of unrelated doctrines and practices, driven primarily by spiritual materialism and a need for personal happiness, will rarely result in the type of thoughtful, informed, and disciplined spiritual fluidity visible among people like Sita Dookeran, Ruben Habito, Marie Romo, VG, and Carlos Alejandro. Responsible religious multiplicity rarely happens in isolation; it requires ongoing conversation with living religious communities. "*Borrowing from* is done best when *learning with*," says theologian John Thatamanil; otherwise, he says, practitioners risk commercializing spiritual disciplines, religious objects, and ritual practices.[10]

Thatamanil suggests several criteria for evaluating complex religious bonds: Do they lead to flourishing? To liberation? Do they "generate knowledge of ultimate reality" that is "otherwise . . . inaccessible"?[11] To these criteria I add, Does a particular instance of spiritual fluidity preserve the richness of images of God and the divine found in sacred texts and practices? Does it account sufficiently for the complexity and messiness of life? Does it turn us outward, away from narcissistic concerns and toward mutuality, to privilege the well-being of others and of creation? Does it promote human freedom and responsibility?[12] Does it, in the words of psychologist Jorge Ferrer, foster the integration and blossoming of all dimensions of a person?

PROBABLE OUTCOMES

While we should evaluate particular instances of spiritual fluidity, we also need to consider the question of spiritual fluidity's potential outcomes on a larger scale: If complex religious bonds continue to increase, where might they lead us? What is their likely influence on the future of religion and spirituality?

What Burke says about the future of cultural hybridity seems to apply equally to complex religious bonds. First, monoreligious identities are not likely to disappear. Individuals and congregations affiliated with single religious traditions will persist; these people and organizations are too prevalent in public life, literature, scholarship, and popular culture to become extinct. But beyond serving as historical artifacts from which spiritually fluid people construct new personal and communal forms of spirituality, monoreligious traditions will probably become less common and less valued in the coming decades. No doubt, religious institutions will defend singularity at formal and doctrinal levels, but such efforts won't matter much to the person on the street. Monoreligious identities will remain important, but increasingly marginalized.

Nor can rigid segregation of religious traditions be sustained. Monoreligious traditions will not successfully isolate themselves from religious pluralism and spiritual fluidity. Too many people—including those who sit faithfully in the same Christian pew on Sunday or bow toward Mecca in the same mosque on Friday or make offerings at the same Buddhist temple week after week—continue to seek religious and spiritual options from other traditions. Religious segregation might continue in institutional and functional forms, but not in everyday life and communal settings. All religions are constantly edited, refined, expanded, reformed, and reconstructed, intentionally or not, as people incorporate ideas and practices from a variety of traditions into their own religious lives. Spiritually fluid practices, identities, and communities will continue to be a norm.

Other outcomes are more difficult to predict, even as spiritual fluidity becomes more popular, more visible, and more influential. Burke faced a similar challenge at the end of his seminal text *Cultural Hybridity*, where he identifies four possible outcomes of globalization and cultural hybridity: homogenization, resistance, local dialect, and synthesis.[13] Burke's categories and analysis are useful to analyze the future of spiritual fluidity, especially if religious singularity shifts to the margins and segregated religious communities fail to thrive.

Spiritual fluidity seems unlikely to cause religious homogenization, a process in which religious boundaries expand, overlap, and eliminate differences until local belief and practice simply reflect an amorphous, universal spirituality. This type of *one-world spirituality*, melding different spiritual and religious ideas, would be continually undermined. People consistently and creatively adapt religious and spiritual ideas, renegotiating their meanings and functions.[14] Religion doesn't remain static long enough for a universal, global spirituality to emerge, and Mystery itself preserves diversity by disrupting religious and spiritual uniformity. Mystery's complexity ensures that something new and different can always emerge. Likewise, resistance to spiritual fluidity seems like a lost cause. The most effective type of resistance might treat spiritual fluidity as a tactic people use to achieve certain ends—not a tool like a screwdriver or hammer, exactly, but a resource like music, visual arts, and other creative activities that seek to entertain, enlighten, and transform people. In this view, people can deploy religious and spiritual resources in any combination for a particular purpose while claiming that the traditions aren't really different but come from—and lead to—a single transcendent source. This approach allows dominant religious traditions to appropriate and subsume the beliefs and practices of minority traditions, then exclude their adherents to create a monopoly on sacred space and religious truth.

But, like homogenization, this type of resistance faces constant erosion from hybridization and multiplicity. Spiritual fluidity refuses to be co-opted by individual, institutional, or commercial powers; it morphs and shifts to undermine religious and spiritual colonization, exploitation, and the promotion of monolithic identities and realities. Local idiom always supplements formal and dominant traditions, as described below, making spiritual fluidity impossible to control or co-opt. "Resistance," Burke says, "is doomed to ultimate failure in the sense that the aims of the resisters, to halt the march of history or to bring back the past, are unattainable."[15]

A more likely outcome is probably the continued growth of local religious idioms, vocabularies of spiritual fluidity that exist alongside formal monoreligious language and traditions. Most spiritual fluidity in history survived as a colloquial practice, clothed in the garments of "official" religion. (Think about Aztecs in Mexico using Catholic doctrine and imagery to mask their ongoing indigenous religion.) Most spiritual fluidity in North American and Europe today also functions this way. Monoreligious traditions and institutions receive formal recognition and can establish a credible, formal religious ethos, whereas colloquial spiritualities thrive among them in secret, usually passing as orthodox. Few "ordinary believers," as Lartey notes, live by official doctrine; their spiritualities express a "mixed pragmatism" of orthodox and heterodox ideas—a description that perfectly fits spiritually fluid people who participate in monoreligious communities. Terms and ideas shaped by spiritual fluidity as a local, colloquial spiritual language usually supplement—and sometimes replace—a formal religious ethos. For me, this type of spiritual fluidity seems most likely and most robust; it preserves the differences among religions while permitting people to accept and use religious truths from outside a given tradition. But idiomatic spiritually can also render spiritual fluidity invisible or frame it as exceptional, constraining its ability to contribute to human flourishing.

Synthetic spirituality—religious expressions that combine traditions to create a new approach that no longer resembles or preserves features of its original sources—also seems possible, but less frequent, as multiplicity increases. Synthesis probably represents a less critical, less disciplined approach to spiritual fluidity—the type of complex religious bonds I criticized above as a mash-up driven by spiritual materialism and focused on personal happiness. Synthetic spirituality borrows from multiple traditions without staying in conversation with them as living communities; it often rejects the norms of the source traditions, refusing to be held accountable for how it transgresses the integrity of particular religions. Some observers view synthetic spirituality as a way of challenging or breaking limits and, in the process, creating new possibilities; others see it as chaotic and impure, the result of unacceptable compromise.[16] Synthetic spirituality should be carefully evaluated against the criteria identified above (and those yet to be articulated). It can be generative and life-giving when it offers new religious forms, promotes transformation, and leads to different ways of imagining and experiencing Mystery—all while remaining accountable to the source's traditions without doing violence to their wisdom and values. But synthetic spirituality is not likely to be a primary outcome of increased spiritual fluidity.

PROVOCATIONS

In the end, I think complex religious bonds are a good thing. They offer much to individuals and to humanity as a whole, inviting us to expand the ways we think about Mystery, its relationship to humanity, and how communities can respond. Below, I suggest some what-ifs for shared reflection. But first, I want to name the most important religious insights I've gained from spiritually fluid people.

First, we don't need to fear Mystery's response to our complex religious bonds. It seems to me that Mystery isn't threatened by, and certainly doesn't condemn, our explorations and deviance from received tradition. Mystery seeks people who seek Mystery. Yes, living a spiritually fluid life has its challenges, but it does not in itself endanger the soul, disappoint God, lead to punishment, contribute to delusion, or separate us from the Mercy flowing without limit through the cosmos.[17]

Second, we should not conflate religious traditions with Mystery. It's tough to tell sometimes, but we do not worship, and are not made whole, liberated, or perfect, by Buddhism, Christianity, Islam, paganism, Ifá, or any other religious system. Only Mystery sets us free, and our traditions are not God. At best, they reflect a partial glimpse of ultimacy (or ultimacies)—glimpses drawn from human experiences of Mystery and codified in doctrine, tradition, and sacred text. When we launch a strong defense of the religious and spiritual truths of a singular religious tradition, we are not defending Mystery; we are defending only a limited interpretation of it. (I should also clarify: Mystery doesn't need our protection. Don't flatter yourself.) Third, if Mystery needs no protection, neither do our religious traditions. They are secondary to the people and communities that nurture us and that we nurture. When religious tradition harms someone, that person takes precedence over the integrity of tradition. Spirit moves through our connections and our differences, spilling over the edges of monoreligious traditions. People need more care than traditions do. Traditions are not beings, but tools to facilitate our relationship with Mystery and with each other.

Having said those things—don't fear Mystery, don't try to protect it, and put people before tradition—I'll now offer some provocations.

What if our spiritualities aren't singular, static, or eternal because Mystery itself—while consistent—is never static?

What if Mystery doesn't reject fluidity but enjoys, engages, revels in, and dances with our spiritual choices, inheritances, collaborations, and multiplicities, celebrating and responding to anything and everything that leads people to glorify and enjoy transcendence with creativity, wonder, fearlessness, and concern for creation?

What if Mystery joyfully responds to our fluidity by meeting us where we are, in whatever form allows us to perceive and receive its presence and actions? What if, when we cross religious lines, Mystery does too? (After all, "as we love God," says Francis Clooney, "God adjusts and comes to us accordingly; if someone loves like a bride, God comes as a groom.")[18]

What if Mystery can be trusted to correct and redirect our complex religious bonds if they become harmful to self or others?

What if spiritually fluid people, encountering Mystery's playfulness, can see and engage in what Thatamanil calls "transformative religious possibilities unavailable to those who inhabit only a single tradition"?[19]

What if the relational, coherence-in-complexity of spiritual fluidity turns out to be the richest way to glorify and enjoy God?

What if it's more important to celebrate connections and relationships than to maintain doctrinal purity or protect historical traditions?

What if insisting on monoreligious identities and practices for the sake of religious tradition hides and erases our deep relationships and connections?

What if naming and claiming complex religious bonds is a way of exposing relational violence and maintaining connection and complexity?

What if it's not enough to see, notice, and name religious multiplicity? What if we need to care for it, too?

And finally, what if Aloysius Pieris is correct when he says, "What saves is love lived out in life, and not necessarily the knowledge of Who that Love is"?[20]

A NOTE
ON METHODS

Many generous people over the years have shared with me their experiences of being spiritually fluid. To protect their privacy, I have changed names and identifying details throughout the book. In some cases, I use my own observations and memory to fictionalize conversations and encounters without claiming to know things about other people—things such as meanings, motives, or thoughts, none of which I can know without asking. These practices are consistent with accepted methodologies for autoethnographic research, as described below.

I wrote *When One Religion Isn't Enough* in part to strengthen the social-scientific understanding of multiple religious bonds. In doing so, I want to move beyond individualistic assumptions to highlight the social dimensions of religious multiplicity. I also wanted to propose a metatheory—an overarching perspective—that could do three things: speak across academic disciplines; highlight the fact that multiple religious bonds have multiple origins, even for one person; and acknowledge how spiritually fluid identities emerge and morph through speech and behavior as well as through thought and choice.

The book isn't scientific in a strict sense; it doesn't report concrete facts about religious multiplicity to prove or disprove a hypothesis. Nor am I proposing a theory that can be validated, generalized, proven, or evaluated by its fidelity to "reality" as measured and experienced by others. The book offers a particular account of religious multiplicity, one story (of myriad possibilities) about what it's like and what it means to be spiritually fluid. I hope it's a fair account, meaning that spiritually fluid people will recognize their own perspectives at least to some degree. I think my account is authentic—ontologically, generatively, tactically, and conciliatorily—and I'll be proven right or wrong to the extent that it:

- raises awareness and leads to more complex understandings of religious multiplicity among scholars, religious leaders, and spiritually multiple people;
- improves the lives of religiously multiple people and their families;
- leads to wise, compassionate, and life-giving action— spiritually, religiously, socially, and politically;
- seems believable, possible, and congruent with life as readers experience it; and
- helps spiritually fluid people articulate who they are to people different from themselves.

As scholarship, the book does not focus on an objective truth that corresponds with an external reality. Its validity depends on its ability to address problems of representation, honor differences and uncertainties, include multiple voices, stimulate engagement and self-reflexivity, and motivate ethical behavior. My concerns are pragmatic rather than representational or predictive: What does this theory allow us to do, to create, to shift? How does it contribute to liberation and freedom? Whose liberation and freedom does it serve? How can it change conversations, language, responses, and responsiveness? Is it beautiful, elegant, or delightful? Does it have rhetorical power, and if so, toward what end?

As a scholar, I use three primary criteria to evaluate my

writing and practice: the promotion of abundant life, the relief of suffering, and *cura anima* (or "the cure of souls" in the Christian traditions). The three are closely related. For example, practicing the cure of souls requires that I avoid harm, resist exploitation, and attend holistically to all of a person's life. The relief of suffering requires that I help people see things clearly, thereby contributing to wisdom, compassion, reconciliation, and peaceful communities. And cultivating abundant life leads me to ask, To what extent does this work give life to people who are silenced, marginalized, or erased by dominant religious communities? To what extent does it increase their agency and clarify their understanding of themselves, their voices, and their presence? To what extent does it provide a location from which to claim their experiences as legitimate and even authoritative?

To meet these criteria, I chose two qualitative methods of research for this project. The first (and predominant) is narrative research, which involved listening to and analyzing the stories of five spiritually fluid people. In hour-long interviews, I asked questions to elicit rich descriptions of their experiences; to identify the existential, relational, and institutional complexities of their religiously multiple lives; and to identify theoretical constructs toward a more structured understanding of complex religious bonds. Some participants chose pseudonyms to be used in the book; others chose to use their legal names. By combining thematic analysis and elements of constructive grounded theory, I analyzed transcripts of these stories to identify shared experiences and common seasons of these spiritually fluid lives. What I learned cannot be generalized to all religiously multiple people, and generalities were not my intention. I wanted instead to evoke detailed stories that can be compared, contrasted, and put into conversation with theoretical ideas about complex religious bonds. I paid attention both to similarities and to significant differences among my research partners, and all participants had the opportunity to review, clarify, and correct what I had written about them. I wanted to provide an account of complex religious bonds using the words of these spiritually fluid people, sticking closely to how they describe and account for their lives. As a second, supplemental approach, I turned to autoethnography. This practice weaves a researcher's stories and experiences with existing theories to describe and analyze personal experience as an avenue toward understanding broader cultural phenomena. What happens to us day by day can illuminate cultural meanings in significant ways that are useful to others. Those meanings must fit how self and others experience life. They must also illuminate social trends or events. By telling my stories as a spiritually fluid person, I hope to encourage others to construct and tell their own stories of complex religious bonds and then compare and contrast their experiences with mine. The autoethnographic parts of the book take a realist approach to the method, seeking to identify how spiritually fluid people know what they know, to help others gain that knowledge, and to identify some of what multiple religious bonds mean in North America during the twenty-first century.

This type of research seeks to convey meaning rather than report facts. To evaluate this type of research, scholars focus not on scientific validity but on the project's verisimilitude (that is, whether it is lifelike, believable, and possible); its communication of existential and experiential truth; and the project's ability to evoke particular situations and settings (among other criteria). My understanding of autoethnography, especially the criteria for its evaluation, is shaped by primarily by Carolyn Ellis, *The Ethnographic I: A Methodological Novel About Autoethnography*, Ethnographic Alternatives 13 (Walnut Creek, CA: AltaMira Press, 2003); Heewon Chang, *Autoethnography as Method*, Developing Qualitative Inquiry 1 (Walnut Creek, CA: Left Coast Press, 2009); Norman K. Denzin, *Interpretive Autoethnography*, Qualitative Research Methods 17 (Thousand Oaks, CA: Sage, 2013); and Patti Lather, "Fertile Obsession:

Validity after Poststructuralism," *Sociological Quarterly* 34 (1993): 685–86. There are many approaches to autoethnography; my choices (and, no doubt, my errors) reflect my own understanding of this practice.

Given diverse academic approaches to these issues, it seems wise to describe my own background and approach. I am by training a pastoral theologian, someone who seeks to understand the richness and complexity of human experiences and then to respond with appropriate, faithful, and effective acts of spiritual care. The object of my discipline is the care that religious people extend to one another and to all creation; pastoral theologians clarify our ethical responsibilities for care, develop effective practices of care, and reflect on caring encounters to construct new theological understanding. For my own work, a primary conversation partner is the psychological metatheory of social constructionism; it invites me to ask "not what goes on 'inside' people, but what people go on inside of."[1] For pragmatic reasons, I tend to use David Tracy's mutual critical (or revised) correlational method to place different academic disciplines into conversation. In seeking to understand and respond to human experience, I privilege liberation theologies and the norms of justice, love, and wisdom as articulated by Immanuel Kant and Michel Foucault. In short, I seek to reduce suffering and increase life's abundance. My practice as a spiritual director and spiritually integrative psychotherapist seeks to promote practices of freedom for all people, and that's one of my motivations for this book.

ACKNOWLEDGMENTS

In June 2014, the Canadian radio host Mary Hynes invited me to talk about complex religious bonds on her show *Tapestry*. Minutes after it aired, I began to receive e-mails from Canadians wanting to talk about spiritual fluidity. Some asked for resources; others sought affirmation. Many hoped to connect to other spiritually fluid people. Some voiced gratitude for finally having a name for a part of their lives they had hidden from family, friends, and spiritual leaders. This correspondence convinced me to write *When One Religion Isn't Enough*. The book is my response to the hunger of spiritually fluid people who want and need to connect with others who share and understand their experiences.

The book took root and matured in a remarkable ecology of scholars, students, religious leaders, and ordinary folk who live with complex religious bonds. I thank the spiritually fluid women and men who trust me as their psychotherapist, spiritual director, colleague, teacher, and religious leader. Their stories serve as cairns, or trail markers, through the territory of religious multiplicity. As I wrote, their experiences kept me from losing my way. Those stories also guarded against—as much as possible—the ways I could distort, exploit, or idealize spiritually fluid lives. My goal was an honest, lifelike, accountable, and relational book that will be measured against the lives of spiritually fluid people.

But the book can only offer an interpretation—my interpretation—of what it's like to be spiritually fluid. All writers have an agenda; that agenda inevitably distorts how they interpret people and events. I'm certain my intentions fail in ways I can't even see. I trust that spiritually fluid people will hold me accountable, both for what's here and for what's not included. Their candid appraisals make me a better writer, pastor, and scholar, and I'm indebted particularly to those I interviewed for the book: Carlos Alejandro, Sita Dookeran, VG, Ruben Habito, and Marie Romo. They reflected on their experiences with grace, wonder, vulnerability, and humor, enriching my understanding of the diversity of complex religious bonds.

I'm grateful also for relationships that sustain my work. Above all, I bow deeply, forehead to the ground, to Karee and Ben, my wife and son, who tolerated the ways this project consumed attention, energy, and other resources. For several years, the book kept me preoccupied, unavailable, and often out of touch with things important to the people closest to me. I was absent, physically and mentally, during homework, walks, soccer games, household maintenance, and vacations. I left dirty dishes in the sink and Popsicle sticks on the couch. I forgot to take my laundry out of the dryer. And yet, these beloved companions put up with it and with me. Especially, they celebrated milestones and reminded me that some things are more important than research and writing.

The curiosity and hospitality of Damian Geddry and Alfredo Galvan helped solidify the project. Lea Appleton, Susan Katz Miller, and Debra Thomas-Zasadzinski reviewed several chapters, and the inimitable Amanda Enayati graciously cheered me on and shared her social capital to advance the proposal. Beyond friendship, Susan Katz Miller has been a conversation partner since we first met in the book exhibit at the American Academy of Religion in 2013; her frequent visits to Claremont are a joy, and her generous enthusiasm and connection to Beacon Press helped make the book happen. David Lott, (former) editor extraordinaire, has been a solid friend and sounding board for years, always willing to say difficult things about writing and scholarship while remaining kind and generous. The members of my writing accountability group—Emily Askew (Lexington Theological Seminary), Eileen Campbell-Reed (Central Baptist Theological Seminary), Allan Cole (The University of Texas at Austin), Mary Moschella (Yale University), Tim Robinson (Brite Divinity School), Janet Schaller (private practice in Memphis), and Frank Thomas (Texas Christian University)—have provided support, humor, and commiseration for more than a decade. Jim Collie provided insight into New Mexico's religious practices. I frequently sat in silence with Chris Michno during the writing of the book. The saints of Claremont Presbyterian Church afforded me a place to live out my Christian commitments.

Further from home, the Benedictine community at Saint Andrew's Abbey in Valyermo, California, provided quiet space, excellent food, and a good vibe for thinking and writing. The Reverend Andrew Green and the congregation of the Church of St. Paul in the Desert in Palm Springs, California, gave me hospitality and a quiet space for work and retreat. The fire tower on Keller Peak provided frequent doses of solitude as well as space for reading and thinking; I'm grateful to tower leader P. J. Smith, the Southern California Mountains Foundation, and the US Forest Service. I completed final edits in the Ahmanson Reading Room of the Huntington Library in San Marino, California, which graciously extended me research and reading privileges. Mike Manning and the staff and regulars at the Last Drop Café afforded me an almost daily dose of sanity, caffeine, conversation, and space for reading. (Mike also tolerated my slothful approach to our family tab.)

One joy (among many) of the community at Claremont School of Theology is a remarkable group of colleagues and students. I am especially grateful to PhD students Katherine

Rand and Josh Morris, both of whom served as research assistants during the project. Katherine has done her own important fieldwork and writing on complex religious bonds in Indonesia, and Josh, in the midst of his own qualifying exams and dissertation processes, cheerfully chased down resources and references, prepared the final manuscript for publication, and completed the index despite my absences and anxiety. Kathleen Greider helps me think about religious multiplicity and the discipline of spiritual care; Monica Coleman provides generative conversation about spiritual fluidity; former communications director Nat Katz helped spread my ideas; and students in the course Buddhist-Christian Thought and Spiritual Care challenged me to think more rigorously and pastorally about the topic. The school provided financial support for transcripts of research interviews, and the president, dean, faculty, and board of trustees granted research leaves that made the project possible; the project emerged during a 2012–2013 leave, and I completed most of the book during my leave in the fall of 2016.

Beyond Claremont School of Theology, I am blessed with smart, funny, curious, reflective, bold, and generous conversations partners. In particular, I thank Victor Gabriel (University of the West) and his husband, Nick Smith; comparative theologian John Thatamanil (Union Theological Seminary in the City of New York); Stephen Graham (Association of Theological Schools); the participants in a two-year Association of Theological Schools consultation on Christian hospitality in a multireligious society; Ruben Habito (Perkins School of Theology, Southern Methodist University); Emmanuel Lartey (Candler School of Theology, Emory University); Francis Clooney (Harvard Divinity School, Harvard University); Paul Knitter (Union Theological Seminary in the City of New York), Alice Keefe (University of Wisconsin–Stevens Point), Judith Simmer-Brown (Naropa University), Sallie King (James Madison University), the late Rita Gross (University of Wisconsin–Eau Claire), and other colleagues in the Society for Buddhist-Christian Studies; Karen Georgia Thompson (United Church of Christ); Anthony Kireopoulos (National Council of Churches); Peniel Rajkumar (World Council of Churches); Karen Hamilton (Canadian Council of Churches); Taos Institute colleagues Miriam Subirana, Ken Gergen, Dian Marie Hosking, Bill Blaine-Wallace, Daniel W. Cho, Brandon McKoy, Amalia Carli, Dawn Dole, and Diana Whitney; and Mary Hynes, Elizabeth Bowie, and Jeff Goodes of Canadian Broadcast Corporation Radio. Anonymous peers who reviewed the proposal also deserve recognition; their questions and suggestions strengthened the book tremendously.

I wrote most of the book while studying in Há Nội, where friends like Guy Dondo, Nguyễn Trường Sơn, Nguyễn Gioi, Nguyễn Bá Duy, and Vũ Hòa sustained me. Nguyễn Tuan Anh, manager of Q. Apartments, replaced my broken writing chair and generally made daily life easier, and doorman Vương Toản kept me laughing.

Scott Anderson created the visual representation of the continuum of complex religious bonds in chapter 5.

Many people listened to and critiqued my ideas during meetings of the Christian Spirituality Group of the American Academy of Religion; the Society for Buddhist-Christian Studies; the Society for Pastoral Theology; the Society for the Study of Christian Spirituality; the World Council of Churches and the United Church of Christ; and the International Association for Spiritual Care at the University of Bern, Switzerland, and at Union Theological Seminary in the City of New York.

In the world of publishing—academic and otherwise—I am grateful to Burke Gerstenschlager; Matt Wise; Tim Robinson and Douglas Christie of *Spiritus: A Journal of Christian Spirituality*; Francis Tiso, Carol Anderson, Thomas Cattoi, Terry Muck, and Rita Gross of *Buddhist-Christian Studies*; and Beth Collins, Susan Lumenello, Perpetua Charles, and Patty Boyd at Beacon Press. And—with a deep bow of respect and debt—I thank Amy Caldwell, executive editor at Beacon Press, who shepherded *When One Religion Isn't Enough* to publication with sympathy, finesse, a sharp eye, and a limited tolerance for authorial BS or self-pity. The care and attention Amy gives not only to the written word but also to the personhood of her authors should be a model—if not a norm—for publishing.

Finally, I am clear that any merit (in the Buddhist sense) from the project belongs not to me but to all these coconspirators and to the abundant life of creation itself, to whom I offer a traditional Zen blessing translated by Kazuaki Tanahashi Sensei and Joan Halifax Roshi:

All awakened ones
throughout space and time,
honored ones, great beings,
who help all to awaken:
Together may we realize
wisdom beyond wisdom![1]

• • • • •

POSTSCRIPT: In February 2017, I was diagnosed with diffuse large B-cell lymphoma. I had already missed the deadline for the book; treatment delayed publication further. I am grateful to a tight-knit group of friends and to my medical team, especially physician Reena Kirtikuma Vora and clinical coordinator Kathleen Bosco, for their patience, humor, support, and expertise. Happily, as of May 2018, I have been in remission for nearly a year and expect to be cancer-free for the rest of my life.

NOTES

Numerous quotes and insights are from my interviews with the following: Carlos Alejandro, Sita Dookeran, Ruben Habito, Marie Romo, and VG. See "A Note on Methods."

INTRODUCTION; OR, WHERE I STAND

1. Quotes from Yann Martel, *Life of Pi* (2001; Toronto: Vintage Canada, 2011), 71, 76.
2. John Blake, "Is Obama the 'Wrong' Kind of Christian?," *CNN Politics*, October 22, 2012, http://politicalticker.blogs.cnn .com/2012/10/22/is-obama-the-wrong-kind-of-christian.
3. Chogyam Trungpa, *Cutting Through Spiritual Materialism* (Boston: Shambhala Publications, 1973).
4. Anglican priest Alan Amos identifies how complex religious bonds challenge institutional religions in "Hybridity: A Personal Reflection," *Current Dialogue* 57 (2015): 50–51.
5. My description of *Mystery* as an inclusive term for the sacred dimensions of life reflects how sociologist Gordon Lynch writes about the sacred, especially in Gordon Lynch, ed., *Between Sacred and Profane: Researching Religion and Popular Culture* (London: I. B. Tauris, 2007); and Gordon Lynch, *The Sacred in the Modern World: A Cultural Sociological Approach* (Oxford, UK: Oxford University Press, 2012).
6. Council on American-Islamic Relations and UC Berkeley Center for Race and Gender, *Confronting Fear: Islamophobia and Its Impact in the United States* (Berkeley, CA: Council on Islamic-American Relations, 2016).

CHAPTER ONE: "NORMAL" SPIRITUALITY?

1. Theologian Michelle Voss Roberts provides a helpful overview of religious multiplicity, especially the dimensions of belief, identity, and practice, in "Religious Belonging and the Multiple," *Journal of Feminist Studies in Religion* 26, no. 1 (2010): 43–62.

2. Paul Knitter, *Without Buddha I Could Not Be Christian*, 2nd ed. (London: OneWorld, 2013), 227.

3. Kelsey Dallas, "What a Mormon Doing Buddhist Meditation Has to Do with the Future of Faith," Religion News Service, July 10, 2017, http://religionnews.com/2017/07/10/what-a-mormon -doing-buddhist-meditation-has-to-do-with-the-future-of-faith; and Lee Hale, "In Salt Lake City You'll Find Mormons Who Meditate," *Weekend Edition Saturday*, National Public Radio, June 17, 2017, http://www.npr.org/2017/06/17/533327601 /in-salt-lake-city-youll-find-mormons-who-meditate.

4. The term *spiritually fluid* grew from my engagement with gender theory, queer theory, and postmodern philosophy. Religion scholar Thomas A. Tweed, however, suggests an "aquatic metaphor" for religion, using the terms *flow* and *confluence*, in his book *Crossing and Dwelling: A Theory of Religion* (Cambridge, MA: Harvard University Press, 2006).

5. I adapted the river metaphor from Hans Alma and Christa Anbeek, "Worldviewing Competence for Narrative Interreligious Dialogue: A Humanist Contribution to Spiritual Care," in *Multifaith Views in Spiritual Care*, ed. Daniel S. Schipani (Kitchener, Ontario: Pandora Press, 2013), 131–47. The river metaphor also appears in World Council of Churches, "Fortresses into Wellsprings: Soothing the Thirst for Spirituality, Affirming Human Dignity," *Current Dialogue* 46 (2005).

6. I learned the date of North America's first Jubu from Emily Sigalow, "Switching, Mixing, and Matching: Towards an Understanding of Multireligiousness in Contemporary America" (presentation, American Academy of Religion Annual Meeting, San Diego, November 22–26, 2014).

7. The political implications of what I call *normal* and *exceptional* types of spirituality are discussed by Indian theologian Sathianathan Clarke in "Religious Liberty in Contemporary India: The Human Right to Be Religiously Different," *Ecumenical Review* 52, no. 4 (2000): 479–89.

8. Patricia Raeann Johnston, "The Church on Armenian Street: Capuchin Friars, the British East India Company, and the

Second Church of Colonial Madras" (PhD diss., University of Iowa, 2015), 196.

9. Statistics about religious participation and mixing religious traditions come from the Pew Forum on Religion and Public Life, "Many Americans Mix Multiple Faiths" (Washington, DC: Pew Research Center, 2009), http://www.pewforum.org/2009/12/09 /many-americans-mix-multiple-faiths; and Theodore Sasson et al., "Millennial Children of Intermarriage: Touchpoints and Trajectories of Jewish Engagement," Maurice and Marilyn Cohen Center for Modern Jewish Studies (Waltham, MA: Brandeis University, 2015). Other empirical data about religious multiplicity come from Gideon Goosen, *Hyphenated Christians: Towards a Better Understanding of Dual Religious Belonging*, Studies in Theology, Society, and Culture (Bern, Switzerland: Peter Lang, 2011); Gideon Goosen, "An Empirical Study of Dual Religious Belonging," *Journal of Empirical Theology* 20 (2007): 159–78; Gideon Goosen, "Towards a Theory of Dual Religious Belonging," in *Ecumenics from the Rim: Explorations in Honor of John D'Arcy May*, ed. John O'Grady and Peter Scherle (Berlin: Lit Verlag, 2007), 237–45; Lori G. Beaman and Peter Beyer, "Betwixt and Between: A Canadian Perspective on the Challenges of Researching the Spiritual but Not Religious," in *Social Identities between the Sacred and the Secular*, ed. Abby Day et al. (Surrey, UK: Ashgate, 2013), 127–42; and Susan Katz Miller, *Being Both: Embracing Two Religions in One Interfaith Family* (Boston: Beacon Press, 2013).

10. For more on the influence of Buddhism in the United States, see Robert Wuthnow and Wendy Cadge, "Buddhists and Buddhism in the United States: The Scope of Influence," *Journal for the Scientific Study of Religion* 43, no. 3 (2004): 363–80.

11. The American scholar J. W. Hustwit explores religious multiplicity as a common experience—a given, rather than a choice—in "Empty Selves and Multiple Belonging: Gadamer and Nagarjuna on Religious Identity's Hidden Plurality," *Open Theology* 3 (2017): 107–16. Finnish scholar Jyri Komulainen also writes about the ubiquity of religious multiplicity, as well as the primarily noncognitive nature of most religion. See his "Theological Reflections on Multi-Religious Identity," *Approaching Religion* 1 (2011): 50–58.

12. For more about normative versus descriptive religious identities, see Richard K. Payne, "Ignorance of the Buddhadharma Is No Excuse: Purser on Monteiro, Musten and Compson," *Critical Reflections on Buddhist Thought: Contemporary and Classical*

(blog), November 29, 2014, http://rkpayne.wordpress.com/2014
/11/29/ignorance-of-the-buddhadharma-is-no-excuse-purser
-on-monteiro-musten-and-compson.

13. Rose Drew, *Buddhist and Christian? An Exploration of Dual Belonging*, Routledge Critical Studies in Buddhism (New York: Routledge, 2011).

14. Canadian scholar Jeanine Diller proposes the categories of voluntary and structural multiple religious participation.

15. See, for example, Janet I. Tu, "Episcopal Priest Ann Holmes Redding Has Been Defrocked," *Seattle Times*, April 1, 2009, http://www.seattletimes.com/seattle-news/episcopal-priest-ann-holmes-redding-has-been-defrocked; and Amy Frykholm, "Double Belonging: One Person, Two Faiths," *Christian Century* (January 25, 2011): 20–23.

16. Mark Tooley, "The Zen Episcopalian: A Buddhist Bishop for the Episcopal Church?," *American Spectator*, April 24, 2009, http://spectator.org/articles/41709/zen-episcopalian; Joel Connelly, "A Buddhist Bishop?," *Seattle Post-Intelligencer*, March 24, 2009, http://blog.seattlepi.com/seattlepolitics/2009 /03/24/a-buddhist-bishop.

17. I used several sources to understand religious violence, conflict, and persecution, especially David Nirinberg, *Communities of Violence: Persecution of Minorities in the Middle Ages* (Princeton, NJ: Princeton University Press, 1996); and Brian J. Grim and Roger Finke, *The Price of Freedom Denied: Religious Persecution and Conflict in the 21st Century* (New York: Cambridge University Press, 2011).

18. John H. Berthrong, *The Divine Deli: Religious Identity in the North American Cultural Mosaic* (Maryknoll, NY: Orbis Books, 1999), 35.

19. Wendy Doniger, "The View from the Other Side: Postpostcolonialism, Religious Syncretism, and Class Conflict," foreword to *Popular Christianity in India: Riting between the Lines*, ed. Selva J. Raj and Corinne G. Dempsey (Albany: State University of New York Press, 2002), xviii, as cited in Johnston, "Church on Armenian Street."

20. Several perspectives on ways that Christians and Jews relate to Buddhism are collected in Harold Kasimow, John P. Keenan, and Linda Klepinger Keenan, eds., *Beside Still Waters: Jews and Christians and the Way of the Buddha* (2003; Boston: Wisdom, 2016).

21. The term *religious multiplicity* encompasses the breadth of being formed by more than one religious tradition without limiting

the focus to identity, belonging, or practice; it is proposed by
my colleague Kathleen J. Greider in "Religious Multiplicity and
Care of Souls," in *Pastoralpsychologie und Religionspsychologie
im Dialog/Pastoral Psychology and Psychology of Religion in
Dialogue*, ed. Isabelle Noth et al. (Stuttgart, Germany: Verlag W.
Kohlhammer, 2011), 119–35. Religion scholar Karla Suomala
prefers "complex religious identity"; see Karla Suomala, "Com-
plex Religious Identity in the Context of Interfaith Dialogue,"
CrossCurrents (September 2012): 360–70. I draw my succinct
description of religious multiplicity from Katherine Rand,
"Deconstructing Religious Identity: A Qualitative Study of the
Spiritually Independent in Java, Indonesia," in *The Insider/
Outsider Debate: New Perspectives in the Study of Religion*,
ed. George D. Chryssides and Stephen E. Gregg (Sheffield, UK:
Equinox Publishing, forthcoming).

22. Olufunmilayo Arewa, "Cultural Appropriation: When 'Borrowing' Becomes Exploitation," *World Post*, June 21, 2016,
http://www.huffingtonpost.com/the-conversation-africa/cultural
-appropriation-wh_b_10585184.html.

23. I stole the term *religi-curious* without apology from editor and former literary agent Matt Wise, email to author, January 8, 2015.

24. Goosen, "Towards a Theory of Dual Religious Belonging," 245.

CHAPTER TWO: CHOOSING

1. Most scholarly writing about complex religious bonds focuses
on human choice, as Teresa Crist aptly describes in "Discuss
ing Displacement: Decolonizing Multiple Religious Belonging,"
Journal of Interreligious Studies 21 (2017): 13–22. This chapter
relies broadly on this choice-oriented work. The best-known text
in this vein is Catherine Cornille, ed., *Many Mansions? Multiple
Religious Belonging and Christian Identity* (Maryknoll, NY:
Orbis, 2002). Gideon Goosen's work informed my approach to
this chapter, especially his understandings of identity, conversion,
and religious symbols: "Towards a Theory of Dual Religious
Belonging"; and *Hyphenated Christians*. Finally, a recent World
Council of Churches volume helpfully expands the discussion of
religious multiplicity beyond US and European contexts. See Peniel
Jesudason Rufus Rajkumar and Joseph Prabhakar Dayam, eds.,
Many Yet One? Multiple Religious Belonging (Geneva: World
Council of Churches, 2016).

2. John B. Cobb, "Multiple Religious Belonging and Reconciliation,"
in Cornille, ed., *Many Mansions?*, 20–28.

3. See Catherine Cornille, "Introduction: The Dynamics of Multiple Belonging," in *Many Mansions? Multiple Religious Belonging and Christian Identity*, ed. Catherine Cornille (Eugene, OR: Wipf and Stock, 2002), 1–6.

4. Nancy T. Ammerman helpfully makes the apparent "spiritual-but-not-religious" dichotomy more complex in "Spiritual but Not Religious? Beyond Binary Choices in the Study of Religion," *Journal for the Scientific Study of Religion* 52, no. 2 (2013): 258–78.

5. Linda A. Mercadante, *Belief without Borders: Inside the Minds of the Spiritual but Not Religious* (Oxford, UK: Oxford University Press, 2014), 236.

6. Elizabeth Drescher, *Choosing Our Religion: The Spiritual Lives of America's Nones* (Oxford, UK: Oxford University Press, 2016).

7. Ibid., 30.

8. Ibid., 38.

9. Ibid., 7.

10. Ibid.

11. Ibid., 14.

12. Berthrong, *Divine Deli*, reflects on immigration and countercultural values (as well as many other topics).

13. Ibid., 17.

14. Elisabeth J. Harris, "Double Belonging in Sri Lanka: Illusion or Liberating Path?," in Cornille, ed., *Many Mansions?*, 77–78.

15. Information about Filipinas who are Christian babaylans comes from my plenary address, "Dis/orientations: Pastoral Counselors, Possibilities, and a Spirit of Skewed Perspectives" (presented at the American Association of Pastoral Counselors, Phoenix, Arizona, April 2, 2011).

16. A variety of texts shaped my understanding of the Christianity missionary project, its relationship to colonialism, and its influence on complex religious bonds. The texts included Werner G. Jeanrond, "Belonging or Identity? Christian Faith in a Multi-Religious World," in Cornille, ed., *Many Mansions?*, 106–20.

17. Martin Palmer, *The Jesus Sutras: Rediscovering the Lost Scrolls of Taoist Christianity* (New York: Wellspring/Ballantine, 2001); and P. Yoshiro Saeki, ed. and trans., *The Nestorian Documents and Relics in China*, 2nd ed. (Tokyo: Maruzen Company, 1951).

18. Michael Amaladoss, "Being a Hindu-Christian: A Play of Interpretations—The Experience of Swami Abhishiktananda," in Rajkumar and Dayam, eds., *Many Yet One?*, 94.

19. Hugo Makibi Enomiya-Lassalle, *Zen: Way to Enlightenment* (New York: Taplinger Publishing, 1968).

20. Devaka Premawardhana, "The Unremarkable Hybrid: Aloysius Pieris and the Redundancy of Multiple Religious Belonging," *Journal of Ecumenical Studies* 46, no. 1 (2011): 76–101.

21. Religious borderlands are geographical, cultural, and psychological places where religious boundaries are challenged. See C. Lynn Carr, *A Year in White: Cultural Newcomers to Lukumi and Santeria in the United States* (New Brunswick, NJ: Rutgers University Press, 2015).

22. Cornille, "Dynamics of Multiple Religious Belonging," 5–6; S. Mark Heim, *Salvations: Truth and Difference in Religions*, Faith Meets Faith Series (Maryknoll, NY: Orbis, 1995); and S. Mark Heim, *The Depth of the Riches: A Trinitarian Theology of Religious Ends*, Sacra Doctrina: Christian Theology for a Postmodern Age Series (Grand Rapids, MI: Eerdmans, 2000).

23. Paul Knitter, quoted in Thomas C. Fox, "Double Belonging: Buddhism and Christian Faith," *National Catholic Reporter*, June 23, 2010, www.ncronline.org/news/double-belonging -buddhism-and-christian-faith.

24. Knitter, *Without Buddha*, 215.

25. Katherine Rand, "Navigating Multiplicity in a Binary World: A Javanese Example of Complex Religious Identity," in Chryssides and Gregg, eds., *The Insider/Outsider Debate*.

26. Pamela Cooper-White, *Braided Selves: Collected Essays on Multiplicity, God, and Persons* (Eugene, OR: Wipf and Stock, 2011).

27. Manuela Kalsky writes about the inevitability of multiple identities in "Embracing Diversity: Reflections on the Transformation of Christian Identity," *Studies in Interreligious Dialogue* 17, no. 2 (2007): 221–31.

28. Sheila Weinberg, "Many Voices, One Mind," *Reconstructionist* (Fall 1994): 53–58.

29. Sallie B. King, "Toward a Buddhist Model of Interreligious Dialogue," *Buddhist-Christian Studies* 10 (1990): 121–26. Note that the insistence on a single worldview that is neither Buddhist, Christian, nor Buddhist-Christian is a hallmark of Rose Drew's empirical study of multiple belonging.

30. For more on Iyanla Vanzant, see Monica A. Coleman, "Iyanla Vanzant: Black Women's Spirituality and the Oprah Effect," Antoinette Brown Lecture at Vanderbilt University, 2016, https:// www.youtube.com/watch?v=b8J9R44UYEU.

31. Kalsky, "Embracing Diversity."

32. Manuela Kalsky and Frieda Pruim, *Flexibel Geloven: Zingeving Voorbij de Grenzen van Religies* (Netherlands: Skandalon, 2014).

33. Karen Georgia Thompson, "Multiple Religious Belonging: Erasing Religious Boundaries, Embracing New Ways of Being," in Rajkumar and Dayam, eds., *Many Yet One?*, 57.

34. Cornille, "Dynamics of Multiple Religious Belonging," 4. Cornille further critiques the idea of multiple religious belonging in "Double Religious Belonging: Aspects and Questions," *Buddhist-Christian Studies* 23 (2003): 43–49.

35. Berthrong, *Divine Deli*, 51. Berthrong's ideas about religious truth are grounded in the thought of American philosopher Justus Buchler, who grew up in a Jewish household and understands the universe as a network of relations.

36. Ibid., 67.

37. Ibid., 65.

38. Drew, *Buddhist and Christian?*, 161.

39. Ibid., 131.

40. Berthrong, *Divine Deli*, 52–53, 65.

41. Peter C. Phan, *Being Religious Interreligiously: Asian Perspectives on Interfaith Dialogue* (Maryknoll, NY: Orbis Books, 2004).

42. The warning about Peter C. Phan's scholarship is Committee on Doctrine of the United States Conference of Bishops, "Clarifications Required by the Book *Being Religious Interreligiously: Asian Perspectives on Interfaith Dialogue* by Reverend Peter C. Phan," United States Conference of Catholic Bishops, December 7, 2007, www.usccb.org/about/doctrine/publications/upload/statement-on -being-religious-interreligiouly.pdf.

43. Simone Sinn, "Vulnerability and Agency in Multiple Religious Belonging: Or, Why God Matters," in Rajkumar and Dayam, *Many Yet One?*, 67.

44. Julius-Kei Kato, "Talking Back to Our Parents: What Asian-North American Hybridity Can Suggest Theologically Back to Asia," in Rajkumar and Dayam, eds., *Many Yet One?*, 176.

CHAPTER THREE: RECEIVING

1. Jan Van Bragt, "Multiple Religious Belonging of the Japanese People," in Cornille, ed., *Many Mansions? Multiple Religious Belonging and Christian Identity*, 7–19; Horatio Clare, "Spirited Away," *Travel and Leisure* (July 2016): 150–68; Jake Wallis Simons, "The 'Catholic Witchdoctors' of Bolivia: Where God and Ancient Spirits Collide," *CNN Travel*, September 17, 2014, http://www.cnn.com /travel/article/catholic-witchdoctors-of-bolivia/index.html.

2. David N. Gellner and Sondra L. Hausner, "Multiple versus

Unitary Belonging: How Nepalis in Britain Deal with 'Religion,' "
in Day et al., eds., *Social Identities between the Sacred and the
Secular,* 75–88.

3. Amaryllis Puspabening, "Bilingual: A Choice of Two Religions,"
   Huffington Post (blog), June 20, 2016, http://www.huffingtonpost
   .com/entry/bilingualachoiceoftworeligions_us_5768a779e4b009
   2652d7e386?.
4. Rand, "Navigating Multiplicity."
5. Komulainen, "Theological Reflections," identifies personal, cultural, and canonical dimensions of religious identity.
6. Miguel A. De La Torre, *Santeria: The Beliefs and Rituals of a
   Growing Religion in America* (Grand Rapids, MI: Eerdmans,
   2004), 1.
7. Ibid., 1–2.
8. Ibid., xviii.
9. Swati Sharma describes a Hindu-Muslim wedding in "What's
   Religion Got to Do with It?" *Deccan Chronicle,* June 26, 2016,
   http://deccanchronicle.com/lifestyle/viralandtrending/260616
   /whatsreligiongotodowithit.html. Shagufta Kalim writes about the
   challenges of a particular Hindu-Muslim marriage in "The Swing
   of the Pendulum—*Phera* or *Nikaah?*" at *Bonobology.com,* July
   15, 2016, http://www.bonobology.com/marriage/themarriedcouple
   /146theswingofthependulumpheraornikaah.
10. The statistics and some perspectives in this section come from
    Miller, *Being Both,* which celebrates the gifts and possibilities of
    interfaith families, and Naomi Schaefer Riley, *'Til Faith Do Us
    Part: How Interfaith Marriage Is Transforming America* (Oxford,
    UK, and New York: Oxford University Press, 2013), which tends
    to emphasize the difficulties of interfaith marriage.
11. Kimberly Winston, "The Religious Wanderings of Bob Dylan,
    Nobel Laureate," *Religion News Service,* October 13, 2016,
    https://www.onfaith.co/commentary/the-religious-wanderings-of
    -bob-dylan-nobel-laureate.
12. Riley, *'Til Faith.*
13. Miller, *Being Both,* 52–53.
14. Ibid., 226.
15. Abraham Vélez de Cea, "An Alternative Conception of Multiple
    Religious Belonging: A Buddhist-Catholic Perspective," in
    *Buddhist-Christian Dual Belonging: Affirmations, Objections,
    Explorations,* eds. Gavin D'Costa and Ross Thompson (Surrey,
    UK: Ashgate, 2016), 165.

16. I learned about this artifact through a photograph and Facebook post from University of Edinburgh lecturer Joshua Ralston in February 2017.

17. Abby Day writes about the social dimensions of religious belief and identity—especially those rooted in kinship networks—in "Euro-American Ethnic and Natal Christians: Believing in Belonging," in Abby Day et al., eds., *Social Identities between the Sacred and the Secular*, 61–74.

18. Material about multiplicity in Vietnam is available at the Frobenius (Courtney L.) Vietnam Research Collection, McCain Library and Archives, University of Southern Mississippi, Hattiesburg, MS, http://lib.usm.edu/spcol/collections/manuscripts/finding_aids /m396. Frobenius was a US Army veteran and founder of Vietnam-Indochina Tours.

19. Insook Lee, "Theology of Improvisation and Korean People's Multiple Religious Identities," *Spiritus* 15 (2015): 97–103.

20. Charles Buck, "From Adherence to Affinity: Multiple Religious Belonging in Hawai'i," presentation, World Council of Churches/ United Church of Christ Consultation on Multiple Religious Belonging, Cleveland, April 2015, available at *Current Dialogue* 57 (2015): 24–28.

21. Paul Hedges, "Multiple Religious Belonging after Religion: Theorising Strategic Religious Participation in a Shared Religious Landscape as a Chinese Model," *Open Theology* 3 (2017): 48–72.

22. Johnston, "Church on Armenian Street," 213. Johnston's text also provided insights about Hindu reverence at Christian shrines in India.

23. Raimon Panikkar, interview by Henri Tincq, translated by Joseph Cunneen, "Eruption of Truth: An Interview with Raimon Panikkar," *Christian Century* (August 16–23, 2000): 835.

24. Richard K. Payne, "Integrating Christ and the Saints into Buddhist Ritual: The Christian *Homa* of Yogi Chen," *Buddhist-Christian Studies* 35 (2015): 37–48.

25. Sunder John Boopalan, "Hybridity's Ambiguity (Gift or Threat?): Marginality as Rudder," in Rajkumar and Dayam, eds., *Many Yet One?*, 135–48.

26. Parts of this section appeared in a different form in my article "Practicing the Religious Self: Buddhist-Christian Identity as Social Artifact," *Buddhist-Christian Studies* 28 (2008): 3–12.

27. For the delusion of self-existence, see Karl Baier, "Ultimate Reality in Buddhism and Christianity: A Christian Perspective," in

Buddhism and Christianity in Dialogue: The Gerald Weisfeld Lectures 2004, ed. Perry Schmidt-Leukel (Norwich, Norfolk, UK: SCM Press, 2001 5), 204; and John P. Keenan, "A Mahayana Theology of the Real Presence of Christ in the Eucharist," *Buddhist-Christian Studies* 24 (2004): 89–100. For the suffering involved with an insistence on a lasting identity, see Alice Keefe, "Visions of Interconnectedness in Engaged Buddhism and Feminist Theology," *Buddhist-Christian Studies* 17 (1997): 61–76.

28. David W. Chappell, "Religious Identity and Openness in a Pluralistic World," *Buddhist-Christian Studies* 25 (2005): 10.

29. I placed quotation marks around "my" to reflect the Buddhist sense that there's no self to own or have an identity. I could also have put quotation marks around "identities" to reflect that identities don't exist, either. Maybe "my" "identities" would be the most accurate!

30. The *Visudimagga* is a fifth-century manual of meditation from the Tibetan Buddhist tradition that outlines forty possible contemplative paths and describes the contemplation of dying and the encouragement of friendship as the two most suitable objects of meditation. See Dean Rolston, "Memento Mori: Notes on Buddhism and AIDS," *Tricycle: The Buddhist Review* 1 (1991).

31. John L. Bell, *The Last Journey* (Glasgow, UK: Wild Good Publications, 1997).

32. William W. How, "For All the Saints," in *Hymns for Saint's Days, and Other Hymns*, ed. Earl Nelson (1864).

33. James M. Day, "Speaking of Belief: Language, Performance, and Narrative in the Psychology of Religion," *International Journal for the Psychology of Religion* 3 (1993): 213–29. Kenneth J. Gergen addresses the relational dimensions of belief in "Belief As a Relational Resource," *International Journal for the Psychology of Religion* 3 (1999): 231–35; and "Reflecting on/with My Companions," in *Social Constructionism and Theology*, ed. C. A. M. Hermans et al., vol. 7 of Empirical Studies in Theology, ed. J. A. Van der Ven (Leiden, Netherlands: Brill, 2002).

34. The statement about "knowing how" rather than "knowing that" appears in Kenneth J. Gergen, "Warranting Voice and the Elaboration of the Self," in *Texts of Identity*, Inquiries in Social Construction, ed. Kenneth J. Gergen and John Shotter (London: Sage Publications, 1989), 75.

35. Ideas in this section are influenced by Michelle A. Gonzalez, "Who Is Americana/o? Theological Anthropology, Postcoloniality, and the Spanish-Speaking Americas," in *Postcolonial Theologies:*

Divinity and Empire, ed. Catherine Keller et al. (St. Louis: Chalice Press, 2009), 58–78. Information on negotiating different identity boundaries comes from Ann Phoenix and Charlie Owen, "From Miscegenation to Hybridity: Mixed Relationships and Mixed Parentage in Profile," in *Hybridity and Its Discontents: Politics, Science, Culture*, ed. Avtar Brah and Annie E. Coombes (London and New York: Routledge, 2000), 72–95.

CHAPTER FOUR: COLLABORATING

1. My understanding of the collaborative path is shaped by the work of Francis X. Clooney, a Catholic scholar of Hinduism, and transpersonal psychologist Jorge N. Ferrer. See Francis X. Clooney, "God for Us: Multiple Religious Identities As a Human and Divine Prospect," in Cornille, ed., *Many Mansions?*, 44–60. See also Jorge N. Ferrer, *Revisioning Transpersonal Theory: A Participatory Vision of Human Spirituality* (Albany: State University of New York Press, 2002); and Jorge N. Ferrer and Jacob H. Sherman, eds., *The Participatory Turn: Spirituality, Mysticism, Religious Studies* (Albany: State University of New York Press, 2008), 136–37.

2. Thich Nhat Hanh, *The Other Shore: A New Translation of the Heart Sutra with Commentaries* (Berkeley, CA: Palm Leaves Press, 2017), 80.

3. This section is adapted from Duane R. Bidwell, "Enacting the Spiritual Self: Buddhist-Christian Identity As Participatory Action," *Spiritus: A Journal of Christian Spirituality* 15, no. 1 (2015): 105–12.

4. Tilden Edwards, *Spiritual Director, Spiritual Companion: Guide to Tending the Soul* (New York: Paulist Press, 2001), 57.

5. The concept of spiritual symbiosis between religious traditions appears in the works of Sri Lankan theologian Aloysius Pieris. See also Paul F. Knitter, "A 'Hypostatic Union' of Two Practices but One Person?," *Buddhist-Christian Studies* 32 (2012): 19–26.

6. Ferrer and Sherman, introduction, *The Participatory Turn*, 72n155.

7. Ibid., 18.

8. Ibid., 23.

9. Monica A. Coleman, "You Can Have It All: Theorizing Transreligious Spirituality from the Field of Black Studies," David and Marilyn Knutson Lecture at Pacific Lutheran University, Tacoma, WA, October 22, 2014, https://vimeo.com/109862420.

10. For spiritual fluidity as a vocation, see the unpublished essay by

Indian theologian and Jesuit priest Michael Amaladoss, "Double Religious Identity: Possible? Necessary?," n.d., www.christ3000 .net/pdf/DOUBLE%20RELIGIOUS%20IDENTITY.doc. For "a special call to holiness," see Peter C. Phan, "Multiple Religious Belonging: Opportunities and Challenges for Theology and the Church," *Theological Studies* 64 (2003): 495–519.

11. Jacques Dupuis, "Christianity and Religions: Complementarity and Convergence," in Cornille, ed., *Many Mansions*, 61–75.

CHAPTER FIVE: A FIELD GUIDE TO SPIRITUAL FLUIDITY

1. For an example of African American women incorporating African spiritualties into their Christianity, see Monica A. Coleman, "The Womb Cycle: A Womanist Practice of Multi-Religious Belonging," *Practical Matters* 4 (2011): 1–9.

2. Boopalan, "Hybridity's Ambiguity"; and Manuel A. Vasquez, *More Than Belief: A Materialist Theory of Religion* (Oxford, UK, and New York: Oxford University Press, 2011).

3. Joyce Shin, "Hyphenated Life: Mixed Loyalties in Family and Faith" (presentation, World Council of Churches/United Church of Christ Consultation on Multiple Religious Belonging, Cleveland, April 2015).

4. Jhumpa Lahiri, "My Two Lives," *Newsweek*, May 5, 2006, http://www.newsweek.com/my-two-lives-106355.

5. My colleague Monica A. Coleman argues that passing, code-switching, and double consciousness—the three strategies that scholars in African American studies have identified for coping with social multiplicity—are useful for understanding religious multiplicity and can be adopted and adapted by spiritually fluid people to clarify how to live with integrity as religiously multiple beings. See Coleman, "You Can Have It All."

6. W. E. B. Du Bois, *The Souls of Black Folk* (Avenel, NJ: Gramercy Books, 1994).

7. The concept of double consciousness is much contested in African American studies, where it is seen as both a positive strategy and a negative burden. For religious implications of the concept, see Jonathon S. Kahn, *Divine Discontent: The Religious Imagination of W. E. B. Du Bois* (Oxford, UK: Oxford University Press, 2011).

8. Parts of this section are based on Sloan Work and Family Research Network, "Resources for Teaching: Mapping the Work-Family Area of Studies," table 1, "Matrix of Information Domains (9/30/01)," 2001, https://workfamily.sas.upenn.edu/system/files

/imported/downloads/About_Matrices.pdf, which I have adapted
to reflect the experiences of spiritually fluid people.

9. I relied on research from several disciplines to identify some useful terms for spiritual fluidity and to conceptualize how different
types of fluidity are related. The continuum of attraction-behavior-
identity comes from research in human sexuality, especially sexual
orientation (for which researchers have long distinguished between
romantic, emotional, and physical attraction), sexual behavior, and
sexual identity. See especially Lisa Diamond, *Sexual Fluidity: Understanding Women's Love and Desire* (Cambridge, MA: Harvard
University Press, 2009). The idea of degrees of religious multiplicity
is supported by the research of Goosen, "Dual Religious Belonging." Sociologist Emily Sigalow identifies diverse ways of navigating Jewish-Buddhist bonds in "Towards a Sociological Framework
for Religious Syncretism in the United States," *Journal of the
American Academy of Religion* 84, no. 4 (2016): 1029–55.

10. John J. Thatamanil's definition of multiple religious participation
comes from his "Eucharist Upstairs, Yoga Downstairs: On Multiple Religious Participation," in Rajkumar and Dayam, eds., *Many
Yet One?*, 5–26.

11. The term *nightstand philosophy* is my adaptation of Thomas A.
Tweed's term "nightstand Buddhists," by which he meant people
who sympathize with the tradition by practicing meditation, reading popular books on Buddhism, decorating with Buddhist art,
and so forth, but who do not convert or even describe themselves
as Buddhist. See Thomas A. Tweed, "Who Is a Buddhist?," in
Westward Dharma: Buddhism beyond Asia, ed. Charles S. Prebish
and Martin Baumann (Berkeley and Los Angeles: University of
California Press, 2002), 17–33.

12. Amir Hussain, "This United Church of Ours," *UC [United
Church] Observer*, August 2007.

13. My understanding of hybridity is informed both by the postcolonial writings of Homi Bhabha, Gayatri Spivak, Stuart Hall, and
others, and by the political-economic usage of the term. As an
aspect of political-economic globalization, hybridity means that
"traces of other cultures exist in every culture" (Marwan Kraidy,
Hybridity, or the Cultural Logic of Globalization [Philadelphia:
Temple University Press, 2005]).

14. To learn more about the Etherean Mission and Brother Ishmael
Tetteh, see the organization's website http://ethereanlife.com.

15. Drew, *Buddhist and Christian?*, 212; and Rose Drew, "Chasing

Two Rabbits? Dual Belonging and the Question of Salvation/ Liberation," in D'Costa and Thompson, eds., *Buddhist-Christian Dual Belonging*, 30.

16. Drew, *Buddhist and Christian?*, 162.

17. Ibid., 212.

18. John J. Thatamanil, "Binocular Wisdom: The Benefits of Participating in Multiple Religious Traditions," *Huffington Post*, February 26, 2011, https://www.huffingtonpost.com/john -thatamanil/binocular-religious-wisdo_b_827793.html.

19. Jonathan Homrighausen, "Spiritually Bilingual: Buddhist-Christians and the Process of Dual Religious Belonging," *Buddhist-Christian Studies* 35 (2015): 57–69.

20. This metaphor is discussed in Harris, "Double Belonging in Sri Lanka."

21. For reflection on spiritually fluid people who are religiously bilingual from birth, see Miller, *Being Both*, 111; and Susan Katz Miller, "Being 'Partly Jewish,'" *New York Times*, October 31, 2013, http://www.nytimes.com/2013/11/01/opinion/being-partly-jewish -.html. See also Rhiannon Grant, "Being Fluent in Two Religions," *Journal of the Sociology and Theory of Religion* 1 (2015), e-ISSN 2255–2715, http://sociologia.palencia.uva.es/revista/index.php /religion/article/view/55/pdf_1.

22. Berthrong, *The Divine Deli*, 38.

23. Drew, *Buddhist and Christian?*, 209–15.

24. Ibid., 215.

CHAPTER SIX: OBSERVATIONS, IMPLICATIONS, PROVOCATIONS

1. Readers familiar with the academic discipline of religious studies might recognize a variation of Jonathan Smith's "here, there, anywhere" trope in this opening paragraph; he writes about it in Jonathan Z. Smith, *Relating Religion: Essays in the Study of Religion* (Chicago: University of Chicago Press, 2004).

2. Peter Burke's classic *Cultural Hybridity* (Cambridge, UK: Polity Press, 2009) provided for me a conceptual framework for discerning the possible outcomes of spiritual fluidity's influence on US spirituality. See especially chapter 5, "Varieties of Outcome."

3. Information on religious diversity and immigration comes from the Pew Research Center, "The Religious Affiliation of U.S. Immigrants: Majority Christian, Rising Share of Other Faiths," May 17, 2013, http://www.pewforum.org/2013/05/17/the-religious -affiliation-of-us-immigrants; Douglas S. Massey and Monica

Espinoza Higgins, "The Effect of Immigration on Religious Belief and Practice: A Theologizing or Alienating Experience?," *Social Science Research* 40, no. 5 (2011): 1371–89, https://www.ncbi .nlm.nih.gov/pmc/articles/PMC3629734; and Harriet Sherwood and Philip Oltermann, "European Churches Say Growing Flock of Muslim Refugees Are Converting," *Guardian* (US edition), June 5, 2016, https://amp.theguardian.com/world/2016/jun /05/european-churches-growing-flock-muslim-refugees-converting -christianity.

4. This section is shaped not only by Burke, *Cultural Hybridity*, but also by Richard A. Shweder, *Thinking Through Cultures: Expeditions in Cultural Psychology* (Cambridge, MA: Harvard University Press, 1991).

5. My thoughts on the material dimensions of religion are informed substantially by Vasquez, *More Than Belief*.

6. For examples, see Kate Mayberry, "Third-Culture Kids: Citizens of Everywhere and Nowhere," *BBC*, November 18, 2016, http:// www.bbc.com/capital/story/20161117-third-culture-kids-citizens -of-everywhere-and-nowhere; and Sarah E. Gaither, " 'Mixed' Results: Multiracial Research and Identity Explorations," *Current Directions in Psychological Science* 24, no. 2 (2015): 114–19.

7. Moises Velasquez-Manoff, "What Biracial People Know," *New York Times*, March 4, 2017, https://mobile.nytimes.com/2017/03 /04/opinion/sunday/what-biracial-people-know.html.

8. See these books by Dan P. McAdams: *The Stories We Live By: Personal Myths and the Making of the Self* (New York: Guilford, 1997); *The Person: An Introduction to Personality Psychology*, 5th ed. (New York: Wiley, 2008); and *The Redemptive Self: Stories Americans Live By*, rev. and expanded ed. (Oxford, UK: Oxford University Press, 2013).

9. Emmanuel Y. Lartey, *Postcolonializing God: An African Practical Theology* (London: SCM Press, 2013), 33.

10. Thatamanil, "Eucharist Upstairs," 17.

11. Ibid., 26.

12. My criteria for spiritual fluidity primarily reflect a Christian perspective. They are shaped by the categories and methodology of Don Browning's seminal work, *Religious Thought and the Modern Psychologies: A Critical Conversation in the Theology of Culture* (Minneapolis: Augsburg Fortress, 1987).

13. Interestingly, Burke inherited complex religious bonds from his Catholic father and formerly Jewish mother, but to my knowledge,

he never explored spiritual hybridity as a personal or cultural reality beyond acknowledging its existence as a form of hybridity.

14. Burke, *Cultural Hybridity*, 107–8.
15. Ibid., 111.
16. Ibid., 113.
17. "The Mercy" is Cynthia Bourgeault's name for Mystery. See Cynthia Bourgeault, *Mystical Hope: Living in the Mercy of God* (Cambridge, MA: Cowley Publications, 2001).
18. Clooney, "God for Us."
19. Thatamanil, "Eucharist Upstairs," 25.
20. Aloysius Pieris, "The Holy Spirit and Asia's Religiousness," *Spiritus* 7 (2007): 126–42.

A NOTE ON METHODS

1. John Shotter, *Social Accountability and Selfhood* (Oxford, UK: Basil Blackwell, 1984), 106.

ACKNOWLEDGMENTS

1. Kazuaki Tanahashi, *Zen Chants: Thirty-Five Essential Texts with Commentary* (Boston: Shambhala Publications, 2015), 29.

INDEX

Abhishiktananda. *See* Le Saux, Henri (Dom)
accommodation, 48
active truth, 56
aesthetic or exhibitive truth, 55
Alejandro, Carlos, 88, 132, 140, 160
Amaladoss, Michael, 46, 165n18, 172n10
Ammerman, Nancy T., 165n4
Amos, Alan, 160n4
Arewa, Olufunmilayo, 30, 164n22
assimilation, 48, 66, 73
autoethnography, 149, 152–53

babaylan, 45, 165n15
Bai, 63
belief, belonging, and behavior, 59, 78, 135
Berthrong, John, 44, 55–56, 129, 163n18, 165n12, 167n35, 167n40, 174n22; on three ways of experiencing and recognizing truth, 57
Bill of Rights for People of Mixed Heritage, 70
braided identities, 51
Browning, Don, 175n12

Buck, Charles, 74, 169n20
Burke, Peter, 133, 141–43, 174n2, 175n4, 175n13, 176n14

cafeteria religion, 8, 21
Chen (yogi), 75–76, 169n24
Clooney, Francis X., 116, 146, 171n1, 176n18
Cobb, John B., 164n2
code switching, 58, 110–11, 113, 172n5. *See also* double consciousness
Coleman, Monica A., 172n5
colonization, colonialism, 23, 27, 30, 44–45, 63, 74, 86, 117, 134, 143, 161n8, 164n1, 165n16
constructive grounded theory, 22, 151
continuum of attraction-behavior-identity, 107, 173n9
conversos, 23
Cornille, Catherine, 47, 54, 164n1, 165n3, 166n22, 167n34
cultural appropriation, 29–30, 164n22

177

cultural hybridity, 141, 142,
    173n13, 174n2, 175n4,
    176n14
cura anima (the cure of souls),
    151

Dalai Lama, 7, 30, 56
De La Torre, Miguel, 65–66,
    104, 168n6
Desideri, Ippolito, 17
Diller, Jeanine, 163n14
Dookeran, Sita, 61, 68, 71, 85,
    132, 140, 160
double consciousness, 58–59,
    111–13, 172n5, 172n7
Dovetail Institute for Interfaith
    Family Resources, 70
Drescher, Elizabeth, 42–43,
    165n6
Drew, Rose, 22, 33, 56, 115,
    127–28, 130, 163n13,
    166n29, 167n38, 173n15,
    174n16, 174n23
Dupuis, Jacques, 100, 172n11
Dylan, Bob, 69

Eastern Orthodox, 45
Ellis, Carolyn, 152
Enomiya-Lassalle, Hugo M.,
    46, 165n19
Etherean Mission, 126,
    173n14

Ferrer, Jorge N., 98–99, 141,
    171n1, 171n6
four Fs of contemporary spiritu-
    ality, 42
Francis (pope), 78

Gergen, Kenneth J., 170n33,
    170n34

Goosen, Gideon, 162n9,
    164n24, 164n1, 173n9
Greider, Kathleen J., 164n21

Habito, Ruben, 39, 44, 103,
    132, 140, 160
Harris, Elisabeth J., 44, 165n14,
    174n20
Heart Sutra, 6, 16, 171n2
Hedges, Paul, 75, 169n21
Heim, Mark, 47, 166n22
here, there, anywhere, 174n1
homogenization, 142–43
Homrighausen, Jonathan, 128,
    174n19
Hussain, Amir, 125–26, 173n12
Hustwit, J. W., 162n11
Hynes, Mary, 154

John XXIII (pope), 39

King, Sallie, 51, 166n29
Knitter, Paul, 8, 14, 22, 48–49,
    127, 161n2, 166n23, 166n24,
    171n5
Komulainen, Jyri, 162n11,
    168n5

Lahiri, Jhumpa, 109, 172n4
Lartey, Emmanuel, 140, 144,
    175n9
Lather, Patti, 152
Lee, Insook, 73, 169n19
Le Saux, Henri (Dom) (pseud.
    Abhishiktananda), 45–46,
    165n18
logic of the one, 7–8

Mercadante, Linda, 41, 165n5
Merton, Thomas, 28
Mezvinsky, Marc, 69

micro-aggressions, 32, 57, 60, 113
Miller, Susan Katz, 15, 69–71, 162n9, 168n10, 168n13, 174n21
Moriscos, 23
multiple belonging, 65, 125
multiple or complex identity, 125
multiple participation, 53, 122, 124

narrative research, 151
nightstand philosopher, 124, 173n11
Noah, Joakim, 1
normal spirituality, 13, 17–18, 20, 21, 27, 133–35
Nostra Aetate, 39, 44

Oriental Orthodox Order, 33
orisha, 7, 66, 88, 89
Osage Forest of Peace, 33
oscillation, 130

Panikkar, Raimon, 75, 169n23
passing, 34, 58, 85, 110, 144, 172n5
personal narratives, 139
Phan, Peter, 58, 167n41, 167n42, 172n10
Piaget, Jean, 48
Pieris, Aloysius, 46, 147, 166n20, 171n5, 176n20
Puspabening, Amaryllis, 64, 168n3

Redding, Ann Holmes, 26, 163n15
religious borderlands, 46, 166n21
religious identification, 42, 53

religious multiplicity, 161n1, 162n9, 162n11, 163n21, 173n9; and affinity, 114, 117–18; and collaboration or collaborative pathway, 90–92, 98–99, 171n1; and context, 114, 116–17; and cultural norms, 72–74; and disposition, 114, 118–19; and dual religious practice, 124; and embedding in family and culture, 64, 67, 69; and expression, 114, 118; and hiding and disclosing, 57; and identity, 115–16, 123; and immigration, 43; lessons of, 107–30; norms and criteria for, 140–41; seasons of, 58, 102–106; written accounts of, 102
religious nones, 39, 41–43, 46, 59
reverence of heaven, 73
Riley, Naomi Schaefer, 69, 168n10
river metaphor, 161n5
Roberts, Michelle Voss, 161n1
Rodrigo, Michael, 46
Romo, Marie, 17, 36, 52, 103, 132, 140, 160
Root, Maria, 70

salvation, 6, 17, 24, 47–49, 107, 120–21
seasons of multiplicity, 58, 102–6
Second Vatican Council, 43
Sherman, Jacob H., 99, 171n1, 171n6
Sigalow, Emily, 161n6, 173n9
Sinn, Simone, 58, 167n43
social pathway, 87

spiritual but not religious
(SBNR), 39, 41–42, 46,
111, 122
spiritual hybrids, 65, 106,
176n13
spiritual materialism, 8, 140,
144, 160n3
strategic multiplicity, 44, 134
strategic religious participation,
75, 169n21
Suomala, Karla, 164n21
synthetic spirituality, 144–45

Tetteh, Ishmael Brother, 126,
173n14
Thatamanil, John J., 122, 128,
141, 146, 173n10, 174n18,
175n10, 176n19
Theravada Buddhism, 5, 79
Thompson, Karen Georgia, 53,
167n33

Tracy, David, 153
Tweed, Thomas A., 161n4,
173n11

University of California,
Berkeley Center for Race
and Gender, 160n6

Vanzant, Iyala, 51, 166n30
Velasquez-Manoff, Moises, 139,
175n7
Vélez de Cea, Abraham, 71,
168n15
VG, 92–95, 104, 132, 140, 160
Visudimagga, 170n30

Weinberg, Sheila, 51, 166n28
Whitehead, Alfred North, 4
Willis, Jan, 116

Zalman, Reb, 94